Character Building

Literature-Based Theme Units

Written by Jeri A. Carroll,
Marsha A. Gladhart and Dixie L. Petersen

Edited by Cindy Iutzi
Illustrated by Cara H. Bradshaw

Teaching & Learning Company

1204 Buchanan St., P.O. Box 10
Carthage, IL 62321-0010

This book belongs to

_____

Cover photo by Images and More Photography

Copyright © 1997, Teaching & Learning Company

ISBN No. 1-57310-071-4

Printing No. 98765

Teaching & Learning Company
1204 Buchanan St., P.O. Box 10
Carthage, IL 62321-0010

Table of Contents

Dear Teacher or Parent,

The focus of this book is to provide tools and life skills children need, so they are equipped to make the important decisions that face them when they enter society at a young age. The material introduces children to the concepts of accountability, perception of self, perception of others, actions and their consequences, critical thinking and decision making.

Teaching about behavior, conflict resolution and values bring teachers face to face with the societal issues of personal identification and culture. Because the subject matter lends itself to personal interpretation, it requires teachers to be objective, yet sensitive to students, parents, schools and communities.

Each child is an individual with needs for privacy. The child has ties to an autonomous family structure which is subjective in its view of behavior, conflict resolution and values. In addition, the students' school has its own customized policies and rules which are an extension of the needs and wishes of the child's parents and the community. These policies and rules represent another set of standards with which students are required to comply.

To ensure the understanding with these individuals and groups, make communication a priority. Inform parents about the topics of discussion. If the topics are worked into themes, provide parents with the informational letters included in this material. Assure parents that *the teaching of specific behavior, specific strategies and specify values is* **not** *included in this material.*

Before teaching this material, it is important for teachers to:

- Read each book carefully
- Have a clear knowledge of the key issues and teachable moments in the story
- Have in mind appropriate, open-ended questions to draw responses from students

While teaching this material, it is critical for teachers to remember:

- As children respond, note each response with as little judgmental tone of voice or body language as possible.
- Allow students, whatever their age, to do the stating, discussing, challenging, suggesting and solving. Their answers are correct for their level.
- If teacher suggestions would be beneficial, guide students forward in their thinking.
- Provide students with a response that they are able to understand. Do not offer an adult response that is too advanced.
- Be realistic in discussions and responses with children.

Activities in this book promote self-examination and examination of others.

- character poems
- suggested journal entries
- alternate story
- illustrations
- role playing
- story lines
- critical stopping points
- suggested questions

Sincerely,

Jeri A. Carroll, Marsha A. Gladhart and Dixie L. Petersen

Behavior

When children misbehave at home and in school, it is often because of internal or external conflicts. They have not yet learned, internalized or chosen to use appropriate behaviors for the situation. Conflict resolution skills will help children in social interactions (the potential for external conflict) and when they encounter events which may cause internal conflict.

This material supports teacher efforts in helping children learn the language and skills necessary to resolve conflicts.

When trying to decide what to do about the misbehavior of young children, the situation must be carefully scrutinized and analyzed:

1. Examine the locations where misbehavior is most likely to occur.
2. Make sure appropriate rules are set. Teach the rules.
3. Evaluate the teacher's consistency in enforcing the rules.
4. Try to determine what the child thinks they are doing and why.
5. Tally the frequency and note the time of the behavior.
6. Evaluate the teacher's subjective reactions to the behavior.
7. State the behavior to parents. Ask if the behavior in question occurs at home. Ask how the behavior is handled at home, and ascertain if the method is successful.
8. Either discuss with the student the behavior that is expected, or tell the student what the behavior is that is expected. Inform the student of the consequences of misbehavior. Ask the student what help they need from the teacher in successfully eliminating the misbehavior, in accomplishing their goal.
9. When the problem arises again, enforce the consequences.
10. Help the child reenter the learning situation.
11. Use the steps of conflict resolution and the stories in these books to:
    - Help the child identify the internal/external conflict
    - See the variety of choices available
    - Determine why the choice made was not acceptable
    - Investigate a better choice
    - Discuss the consequences of each possible choice

However, if there is a threat of physical harm in any misbehavior, the misbehavior must be stopped immediately, with appropriate consequences meted out to those involved.

Conflict Resolution

Many problems that occur in schools and homes involve conflicts. They may be internal (ambivalence, choice making, decision making) or external (when one's wants and needs conflict with others' wants and needs). Experienced adults find conflict difficult. Children have even fewer tools and skills. In this book the questions posed to children are similar to those suggested in *Conflict Resolution* (Johnson & Johnson, 1995, pp. 52; 76):

Steps to Conflict Resolution

- Identify the conflict or problem.
- Describe how each person feels and why.
- Examine reasons for each position.
- Try to understand each other's perspective (difficult, if not impossible for young children).
- Tell about different options and their consequences.
- See what the story decision is. Does it match predictions students have made?
- Determine what might have been done in the first place to avoid the conflict.

From Literature to the Classroom

Tolerance and understanding are important in conflict resolution, Sorenson (1992) says. One must assume that each person always makes the best choice available at the time. In their perspective, they may have limited choices. When teachers want to increase the number of choices that children have available, either internal or external conflicts arise.

This book includes stories which present some kind of conflict, either internal or external. Stopping points are suggested as conflicts arise, develop and conclude. In addition, questions are supplied for teachers to ask their students. With their teacher's assistance, children will soon begin to initiate necessary language and strategies to handle everyday conflicts. Capitalize on these newfound strategies by extending them into classroom conflict situations.

There are usually several ways to solve every problem. Sorenson suggests helping children examine alternatives, learn to evaluate, make decisions, use tolerance, let chance decide, share, take turns, compromise, apologize, recognize the validity of another's positions, postpone the decision, interject humor and look for a fresh approach.

Teachers should use their influence wisely.

Values

Teaching values is controversial. Teachers must know students, their parents and community expectations well before teaching about values. In this book, the focus is on seven values upon which most communities can agree: honesty, respect, responsibility, compassion, self-discipline, perseverance and giving (Ernest Boyer, *The Basic School,* 1995). Also included is the all-important virtue of friendship (William Bennett, *The Book of Virtues,* 1994).

Honesty

Children learn to recognize *honesty* in stories where someone "carries out his or her responsibility carefully and with integrity, never claiming credit for someone else's work." In addition, people are willing to acknowledge their own wrongdoing (Boyer, p. 183). Children see other children deciding that honesty is the best policy in books like *Too Many Tamales* (Gary Soto) and *The Empty Pot* (Demi).

Respect

To help children learn about *respect* (each person responding "sensitively to the ideas and needs of others without dismissing or degrading them") try stories like *Frederick* (Leo Leonni) and *The Great Kapok Tree* (Lynne Cherry). These books and others show that "differences among people are celebrated" and "all members of the community are able to accept both praise and constructive suggestions from others. While affirming individual freedom, the rights of the group are also fully honored." (Boyer, pp. 183-184)

Responsibility

In books like *Sachiko Means Happiness* (Kimiko Sakai) and *Swimmy* (Leo Lionni), the child has a sense of duty *(responsibility)* to willingly fulfill the tasks he or she has accepted or has been assigned. Work is conscientiously performed. "Members of the community feel comfortable asking for help and agree that they must be held accountable for their behavior." (Boyer, p. 184)

Compassion

Children learn that people should be considerate and caring in *Mean Soup* (Betsy Everitt) and *Jamaica Tag-Along* (Juanita Havill). In addition, they see that "everyone, from time to time, feels hurt, confused, angry, or sad." Instead of ignoring such conditions they learn that "people reach out to one another." In dealing with conflict, "people seek reconciliation and try to understand each other, even forgive." (Boyer, p. 184)

Self-Discipline

Everyone has limits that are mutually agreed upon and established personally. *Self-discipline* should be exercised in relationships with others, "especially in the way people speak to one another. *Self-discipline* also applies to the use of time . . . . It reflects habits of good living." (Boyer, p. 184)

Children's books such as *Apple Picking Time* (Michelle Slawson) and *Baby Rattlesnake* (Te Ata) demonstrate the making of personal decisions and seeing the consequences of those decisions on others.

Perseverance

Setting and accomplishing goals are important qualities for children. The goals can be individual, group or class goals. *Perseverance* involves the diligence with which people use the "inner strength and determination to pursue well-defined goals. It does matter that a task be completed once it is begun, and to persevere not only teaches discipline, but brings rewards as well." (Boyer, pp. 184-185)

Read *How Many Days to America?* (Eve Bunting) and *Pancakes for Breakfast* (Tomie de Paola) to help children define the value of sticking to a task until it is complete.

Giving

Young children will discover that "one of life's greatest satisfactions comes from *giving* to others, and will recognize that talents should be shared, through service." (Boyer, p. 185) *The Legend of the Bluebonnet* (Tomie de Paola) tells of a young girl's gift to her tribe. *The Rainbow Fish* (Marcus Pfister) tells of fish giving shiny scales away. "Rather than waiting to be asked, . . . children look for opportunities to respond positively to the needs of others, without expectation of reward."

Friendship

Genuine friendships take time (Bennett, p. 269). Young children see *friendship* differently than adults. Friends are people who happen to be in the same place that they are in, at the same time. Young children don't usually understand the deep and binding affects of friendship. True friendship "usually rises out of mutual interests and common aims. The demands of friendship–for frankness, for self-revelation, for takings friends' criticisms as seriously as their expressions of admiration or praise, for stand-by-me loyalty, and for assistance to the point of self-sacrifice" are all part of friendship. Children can examine the qualities of friendship in *The Velveteen Rabbit* (Margery Williams) and *Jamaica and Brianna* (Juanita Havill).

Conflicts in Children's Books

Children love a good story. Stories are entertaining and challenge the imagination. In stories, children encounter characters who deal with many situations and conflicts similar to those they will face in the real world. In this book, the stories involve characters in the type of conflicts that everyone encounters in life.

One of the most important goals in sharing a book with young children is the mutual pleasure the story brings. Good stories create a positive experience that often leads to a lifetime of reading enjoyment. These stories are part of a shared culture. While reading stories to young children, keep in mind that the pleasure of the story is an important goal. The power of the story may be lost through overdiscussing or overteaching. A valuable opportunity to share the love of reading may be the result.

Good stories influence children's values. Children learn from the characters' thoughts and actions. Through consequences of those actions, different perspectives become apparent. Many adults and children think of the Little Red Hen when someone doesn't do their share of the work. Horton hatching the egg comes to mind when someone takes responsibility too lightly. These stories never lose their power to help children formulate their own concepts of right and wrong.

The carefully selected books in this volume allow children to observe situations from different perspectives that require decision making based on a set of values. The stories stimulate a variety of emotional responses. Those responses lead to personal and social development. Use these books as a part of any reading program.

The books were also selected for their powerful stories and illustrations.

How to Use This Book

Choose a Value

The introductory material describes the values highlighted in this book. Value selection may arise from a parallel situation in the classroom or may be randomly chosen for investigation with the children.

Choose a Story

The bibliography at the end of each value's unit lists suggestions of particular stories to be used for that value. These stories include books, CDs, audiocassettes and/or videocassettes. The story is listed first. If the story appears in other than book form, that form is noted in parentheses ( ). If there is no form listed in parentheses, assume the story is in book form.

Review Suggested Stopping Points and Questions

The reference statement lists the page on which a summary of the story is provided. Also, stopping points, questions and extension activities are included. Before reading to students, review the story (open book). Stop at the suggested stopping points (stop sign **STOP**). Review the questions to predict student responses. Decide on ways the story can be extended in centers or other activities.

Present the Story Using Stopping Points and Questions

Present the story to students stopping periodically to ask questions which demonstrate the steps of conflict resolution. Do not predetermine value judgments for the students. They are not as advanced as adults in value judgement or development. Accept and record their responses quickly.

Complete the Story

At the conclusion of the story, review the original conflict, the decision and the consequences. Also examine what could have happened if the character had chosen a different alternative.

Children's Literature Reproducibles

The reproducibles at the back of this book can be used with any of the stories in this book. Make an overhead, enlarge as a chart, re-create on the chalkboard or give students copies. By using graphic organizers, children see a visual form of the discussion and participate in creating ideas. Use graphic organizers with groups of various sizes and composition. These methods help meet individual needs of students who experience all modes of language and literacy development. The use of these ideas allow children to be actively involved in concrete activity.

Children's Use and Reuse

Place the book, supporting props, CDs and/or tapes where students can continue to explore them.

Dear Parents,

This week we are studying about *honesty,* one of the virtues that Dr. Ernest Boyer suggests schools should examine. Dr. Boyer defines *honesty* as, "Each person carries his or her responsibilities carefully and with integrity, never claiming credit for someone else's work and being willing to acknowledge wrongdoing." He suggests people share ideas openly in a climate of trust, with confidence that what is written and spoken is honestly expressed. Ernest Boyer, before his death late in 1995, served as U.S. Commissioner of Education and was president of The Carnegie Foundation for the Advancement of Teaching.

Several books for young children address *honesty.* These books include:

Bedtime for Frances
A Day's Work
The Empty Pot
Ira Sleeps Over
Sam, Bangs and Moonshine
The Tale of Peter Rabbit
Too Many Tamales

We will read some of these in class.

Expect your child/children to use the words: *honest, honesty, truth* and *trustworthy* in their conversations with you this week. You may have an opportunity to share your feelings with your child/children about *honesty.* Please feel free to call with questions and concerns.

Sincerely,

A Day's Work

Summary

Francisco's grandfather has just moved to California from Mexico. He does not speak English, so Francisco speaks for him and helps him get a job. Problems occur when Grandfather does not know how to do the job. The boss discovers that Francisco was not telling the truth about Grandfather's abilities. Grandfather teaches Francisco a valuable lesson about being honest.

Before Reading

Talk about people not being able to speak the language of the country in which they live.

While Reading

📖 Read to the part of the story in which Ben takes Grandfather and Francisco to the high bank with six big, black trash cans.

🛑 Why is Grandfather worried that Francisco told Ben that Grandfather is a gardener? What could happen?

📖 Grandfather and Francisco begin to work.

🛑 Why is Grandfather so happy and proud of Francisco?

📖 How will they know which are weeds and which are flowers? Later when Ben returns, he yanks off his Lakers cap and slams it against the van.

🛑 Why can't Francisco look at Grandfather when he speaks? What will Ben do? What will Grandfather do?

📖 Finish the story.

🛑 What important things does Ben *not* have to teach Grandfather? What does Francisco learn? What is the result of a lie?

After Reading

What values do students recognize in this story? What other stories are similar to this one? How are they different? What real-life incidents touch on the same issues?

A Day's Work
Extension Activities

Solving the Problem

Using the chalkboard or chart paper, record ideas generated by a discussion.

What is the problem? Analyze what Francisco does. Is it right or wrong? Why? List Francisco's other alternatives in getting Grandfather a job. List the pros and cons of each plan.

Hat Day

The Lakers cap plays a role in the story. Discuss the importance of admiring a team as a role model. Ask students to wear a ball cap (or a T-shirt) with the logo of a favorite team. Provide extras for those who do not have one. Teachers should participate.

Honesty Badges

Create honesty badges from construction paper. Use a badge model for younger students to trace. Students who can, may create their own. Generate ideas by studying the T-shirt and cap logos that everyone is wearing. As a class, write some examples: *Honesty* means "happiness." Being honest is being a friend.

Weeds or Flowers?

Go for a walk on the school grounds and neighborhood to observe plants. Try to decide which ones are weeds and which ones are flowers. A city or school grounds crew worker could visit to discuss the job of maintaining the grounds.

The Empty Pot
A Case of Honesty and Perseverance

Summary

Ping loves flowers and is such a good gardener that anything he plants "bursts into bloom." When the elderly emperor needs a successor, he calls all the children in the land to the palace. They are given special seeds to plant. They are to return to the palace in a year to show the emperor their best attempt. Ping works and works. He tries everything he knows, but the flowers do not grow. He returns in a year with an empty pot. All the other children have beautiful pots of flowers. Because Ping has been honest, he is chosen to be the emperor's successor. You see, the seeds were no good and only an honest person could succeed the emperor.

While Reading

Read to the part of the story in which Ping has planted the seeds and is waiting for them to grow.

STOP What is the problem here? How does Ping feel? What should Ping do? List all the solutions students suggest. Examine the consequences for each of the solutions students suggest.

Read to the point of the story in which Ping is ashamed of his empty pot. His friend suggests he can't go to the Emperor with an empty pot.

STOP Ask the problem-solving questions above with the new information gained from the story.

Read to the part of the story in which the Emperor asks why Ping has brought an empty pot.

STOP Ask the problem-solving questions listed above again. Listen carefully to students' responses. Try not to be judgmental.

Finish the story.

STOP Match students' responses to the author's responses.

After Reading

What values do students recognize in this story? What other stories are similar to this one? How are they different? What real-life incidents touch on the same issues?

14

The Empty Pot
Extension Activities

Class Book

Ask students to illustrate their favorite part of the story using permanent fine-tipped black pens. When the pictures are dry, have children use pastels or watercolors to color their pictures. Then ask students to write the words explaining their favorite part of the story at the bottom. The next step is to put the pages in sequential order. Children will need help stapling the pages into a class book.

Story Alternatives

Ask students to write or illustrate their versions of the story using the stopping points and some of their problem solutions discussed in class. Perhaps they thought Ping should use a different type of soil, fertilizer or water. Ask them to tell that part of the story and finish with the author's ending or another ending. Discuss how the values of honesty and perseverance are played out in their versions.

What's in the Pot?

Give each child an empty pot, a variety of seeds and potting soil. Ask them to plant the seeds. Record their actions, the results and how they feel. Discuss the values students think are manifested in this activity.

Perseverance   Giving   Friendship

Honesty   Respect   Responsibility   Compassion   Self-Discipline

Ira Sleeps Over
Teddy Bear Friends

Summary

Ira is invited to sleep over at Reggie's house. He is excited until he becomes concerned about taking his teddy bear with him. Ira worries that Reggie will make fun of him. He also worries that he won't be able to sleep without his teddy bear. After all his worrying, Ira discovers that Reggie sleeps with a teddy bear, too. So Ira returns home to get his teddy bear for the sleep over.

Before Reading

Discuss things that help you sleep at night. Some people like to cuddle with a blanket or a toy. Some people like to sleep on one side or with a special pillow.

While Reading

📖 Read to the part of the story in which Ira first asks, "Should I take him?"

🛑 What should Ira do? Should Ira leave the teddy bear at home? Why? Should he take the teddy bear? Why?

📖 Read to the point of the story in which Ira and Reggie start to tell ghost stories.

🛑 Discuss why Reggie goes to get his teddy bear. Why doesn't Reggie take his teddy bear in the first place? How does it make Ira feel when he discovers Reggie has a teddy bear, too?

📖 Finish the story.

🛑 Why does Ira's sister think Reggie will laugh at Ira's teddy bear? Why do his parents think it is okay for Ira to take his bear?

After Reading

What values do students recognize in this story? What other stories are similar to this one? How are they different? What real-life incidents touch on the same issues?

Honesty Respect Responsibility Compassion Self-Discipline Perseverance Giving Friendship

16

Ira Sleeps Over
Extension Activities

Oh! So Many Teddy Bears!

Have children bring their teddy bears to school for a day. Weigh and measure the teddy bears. Sit their bears on their laps. Place them in a corner or dramatic play area with props and baby clothes. Let the children play with "Oh! So many bears!" Teachers may supply a few bears if some children do not have one, or any stuffed animal may qualify.

Hospitality

Make a list of things that can be done to make a guest feel comfortable in one's home. Let each child choose an item on the list to act on.

Make a second list of things that can be done to make guests in the classroom feel comfortable. Post the list in the classroom so everyone will remember how to be a good host.

Teddy Bear Tea

Ask students to bring a teddy bear or favorite toy to school for a teddy bear tea. Pretend the toys are real guests and practice good manners. Supply a few stuffed animals for children who do not have one.

Related Readings

To explore difficulties in getting to sleep at night, Russell Hoban's *Bedtime for Frances* is a humorous approach.

Foo Foo Sleeps Over

Fill in the blanks and illustrate each part of the story.

Foo Foo invited Tah Tah to spend the night. Tah Tah was very excited. Foo Foo's mother would fix _____ for their dinner.

Tah Tah knew that later they would have

_____

and _____ for snacks.

Then they would play _____

and _____ .

After that, the two teddy bears would settle down in their beds and tell stories about

_____

When Tah Tah returned home the next morning, Ira would want to hear about all the fun at Foo Foo's house.

18

Sam, Bangs and Moonshine
Being Truthful

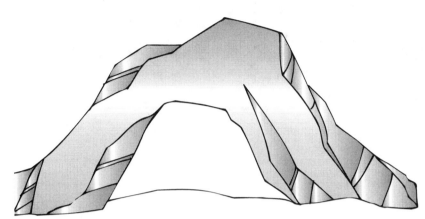

Summary

This 1967 Caldecott winner tells the story of Sam, a fisherman's daughter, who has the reckless habit of lying. She has a cat named Bangs. She makes up stories about Bangs and many other things. Her father tells her to talk "real," not "moonshine." She has trouble understanding what is meant by *moonshine.*

While Reading

Read to the part of the story in which Sam's father leaves to go fishing and she promises to not talk moonshine.

STOP What does her father mean by *not talking moonshine?*

Read to the point of the story in which the prediction is verified and Thomas goes to the cave behind Blue Rock.

STOP What does *moonshine* mean? What would a student expect to hear from a teacher instead of *moonshine?* What do parents say instead of *moonshine?*

Read to the part of the story in which Bangs returns a sodden mess.

STOP Do you think Sam knows the difference between *real* and *moonshine?* Do you think she will continue to talk moonshine? Why?

Finish the story.

STOP Did Sam learn the difference between good and bad moonshine? How do you know?

After Reading

What values do students recognize in this story? What other stories are similar to this one? How are they different? What real-life incidents touch on the same issues?

Friendship Giving Perseverance **Self-Discipline** Compassion Responsibility Respect Honesty

Sam, Bangs and Moonshine
Extension Activities

Real or Moonshine?

Give each child two card-sized pieces of paper. Ask students to draw a "real" event. On the other they are to draw a "moonshine" event.

Prepare a REAL label and a MOONSHINE label. Place the two labels on the floor. Direct students into pairs. Explain the two events that each drew. Don't tell which drawing is real or moonshine and switch cards.

Bring the group together. Put the REAL and MOONSHINE labels on the chalk tray. Each student should bring one event at a time forward. After explaining it, they should put it in the right place.

When the group activity is complete, place the materials in a center where children can continue the activity independently.

On the Old Rug

Ask students to draw a beautiful rug and moon.

Supply an assortment of magazines and catalogs. Ask students to cut out several things that could be on a rug and several things that would not be on a rug. Ask them to cut out the rug and the moon.

In pairs, have students tell their partners what their picture is and let the parent decide whether or not it should be on a rug or whether it is moonshine. Younger children can glue the picture on the rug or moon.

Older children can list the "real" things on the back of the rug and the "moonshine" things on the back of the moon.

Honesty Respect Responsibility Compassion Self-Discipline Perseverance Giving Friendship

20

The Tale of Peter Rabbit
What ever happens to the naughty rabbit?

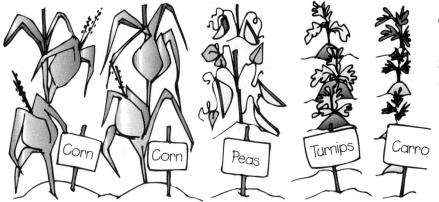

Summary

Mother Bunny had to go out. She told Flopsy, Mopsy, Cottontail and Peter to behave and not to dare go out to Mr. McGregor's garden. But what did Peter do? He just about got caught!

While Reading

📖 Read to the part of the story in which Mrs. Rabbit warns her children to stay out of McGregor's garden and tells them to run along and keep out of mischief.

🛑 What will the little rabbits do? What will happen to them if they do each of the things students suggest?

📖 Read to the point of the story in which Flopsy, Mopsy and Cottontail are good little bunnies.

🛑 What will Flopsy, Mopsy and Cottontail do next? Where is Peter? What will happen to him?

📖 Read to the point of the story in which Mr. McGregor calls, "Stop, Thief!"

🛑 Why does Mr. McGregor call, "Stop, Thief!" What will he do now? What will Peter do? What should Peter do?

📖 Read to the point of the story in which the little mouse carrying peas tells him that she cannot help.

🛑 What does Peter do when his mother tells him to stay away from McGregor's garden? How does he feel now? Whatever can he do?

📖 Read to the point of the story in which Peter escapes home to the big fir tree.

🛑 What will happen to him for misbehaving?

📖 Finish the story.

🛑 Does Peter get punished for disobeying? How? How does he feel? How does Mother feel?

After Reading

What values do students recognize in this story? What other stories are similar to this one? How are they different? What real-life incidents touch on the same issue?

Friendship Giving Perseverance Self-Discipline Compassion Responsibility Respect Honesty

The Tale of Peter Rabbit
Extension Activities

In the Garden

Mr. McGregor's garden has lettuce, French beans, radishes and parsley. Buy packets of those vegetable seeds (with pictures of the vegetables on the packets). Buy some of each vegetable from the grocery store's produce department. With students, examine the seeds, pictures and vegetables. Give everyone a taste of the vegetables. Plant the seeds in rows in a large tub or small garden. Put the vegetable packet on a stick at the end of the row to show which seeds have been planted. Monitor closely for a couple of months.

Bunny Obstacle Course

The bunnies hop down the lane. Peter goes under the gate, around the end of the cucumber frame, all over the garden, into a gooseberry net, into the toolshed, into a can, out of the window, across the garden, on the wheelbarrow, off the wheelbarrow and under the gate.

Ask students to decide ways that represent each of Peter's moves. Organize a hop through the bunny obstacle course.

Older children can draw the course and label each of its parts with prepositional phrases from *The Tale of Peter Rabbit*.

Bread, Milk and Blackberries

Enjoy a snack of bread, milk and blackberries.

Too Many Tamales
The ring was gone. Maria must be honest.

Summary

Maria and her mother are making tamales for a Christmas celebration with the family. Mother takes off her diamond ring, places it on the countertop and goes to answer the telephone. Maria loves that sparkly ring and before she knows it, she has put it on her thumb. Maria begins to knead the dough. Mother returns and sends Maria to get Father to help make the tamales. Only later does Maria remember the ring. She encourages her young cousin to eat the 24 tamales to find the ring. It isn't in the tamales. She decides to go tell her mother. As she begins, she sees the ring on her mother's finger. And now, what to do about the 24 missing tamales!

Before Reading

Discuss the various types of family traditions students partake in for various holidays.

While Reading

📖 Read to the part of the story in which Maria eyes the ring on the countertop.

🛑 What does Maria want to do? What could happen if she does? What should she do?

📖 Read to the point of the story in which Maria remembers about the ring.

🛑 What are the various things Maria could do? What could happen with each solution?

📖 Read to the part of the story in which Maria doesn't find the ring in the tamales.

🛑 What could Maria do? What could happen with each solution?

After Reading

What values do students recognize in this story? What other stories are similar to this one? How are they different? What real-life incidents touch on the same issue?

Honesty   Respect   Responsibility   Compassion   Self-Discipline   Perseverance   Giving   Friendship

Too Many Tamales
Extension Activities

What's in the Dough?

Make a batch of play dough. Hide several objects in the dough. As the objects are found, ask students to put them in a bowl.

After each student has had a chance to retrieve five objects from the dough, have them draw a picture of the five objects on paper that are the same color as the dough. Display the pictures in the center. Hide the objects in the dough again. Ask students to hunt for specific objects they see in the pictures.

Two Tamales

Bake tamales with help from a parent and students. Discuss good hygiene as they make the dough and wrap the tamales. Make the tamales small enough so that each child gets two.

Corn

Look at the corn plant. Take the husk off the outside of the ear. Boil the ear to eat. Save the husk to see if it looks like the husks that are on the outside of the tamales.

Cornhusks

Save and dry the husks from several ears of corn or purchase some cornhusks at the grocery store. Ask students to wrap objects in the husks. If the husks are too brittle, soak them until they are flexible.

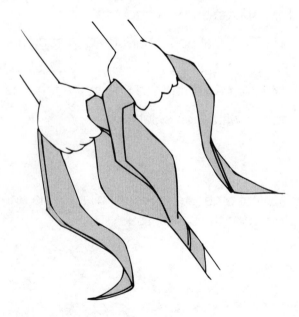

Bibliography

Bunting, Eve. (1994). *A Day's Work.* Ill. Ronald Himler. New York: Clarion Books. ISBN: 0-395-67321-6

Demi. (1990). *The Empty Pot.* New York: The Trumpet Club. ISBN: 0-440-84476-2

Hoban, R. (1960). *Bedtime for Frances.* New York: Harper. ISBN: 0-06-022351-0

Ness, Evaline. (1966). *Sam, Bangs and Moonshine.* New York: Henry Holt and Company, Inc. ISBN: 0-440-84669-2

Potter, Beatrix. (1902). *The Tale of Peter Rabbit.* London: Frederick Warne & Co. ISBN: 0-7232-3460-4 (Many editions available.)

Potter Beatrix. (1988). *The Tale of Peter Rabbit.* (audiocassette). New York: Warner Juvenile Books.

Soto, Gary. (1993). *Too Many Tamales.* Ill. Ed Martinez. New York: G.P. Putnam's Sons. ISBN: 0-399-22146-8

Waber, Bernard. (1972). *Ira Sleeps Over.* Boston, MA: Houghton Mifflin Company. ISBN: 0-395-20503-4

Waber, Bernard. (1987). *Ira Sleeps Over.* (audiocassette). Brilliance Corporation.

Waber, Bernard. (1985). *Ira Sleeps Over.* (videocassette). BFA Educational Media.

Dear Parents,

This week we are studying about *respect,* one of the virtues that Dr. Ernest Boyer suggests schools should examine. Dr. Boyer defines *respect* as "Each person responds sensitively to the ideas and needs of others without dismissing or degrading them. Differences among people are celebrated, and all members of the community are able to accept both praise and constructive suggestions from others. While affirming individual freedom, the rights of the group are also fully honored." Ernest Boyer, before his death late in 1995, served as U.S. Commissioner of Education and was president of The Carnegie Foundation for the Advancement of Teaching.

Several books for young children address *respect.* These include:

Alexander and the Wind-Up Mouse
Are You My Mother?
The Big Boasting Battle
Fish Is Fish
Frederick
The Hating Book
I Hate My Brother Harry
Inch by Inch
The Quarreling Book
Smoky Night
Stellaluna

We will read some of these in class.

Expect your child/children to use terms like *respect, rights, needs, degrade, accept* and *constructive suggestions* in their conversations with you this week. You may have an opportunity to share your feelings with your child about *respect.* Please feel free to call with questions and concerns.

Sincerely,

The Big Boasting Battle
Being Perfect but Different

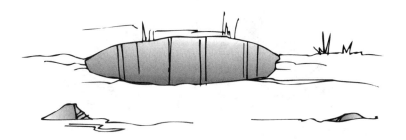

Summary

Horace the lion and Sylvester the snake are friends, but they argue. During a big boasting battle, a problem occurs that can only be solved by them working together.

Before Reading

Show the cover and ask students to predict why the lion and the snake are pointing at themselves. Discuss the meaning of *boasting*.

While Reading

📖 Read to the part of the story in which the two friends try to impress each other and Sylvester finally swims across the river.

🛑 Why is Horace angry in the beginning? What problems are caused by someone being late? What are some ways a person who is often late could help overcome the problem? Discuss some of the ways they try to impress each other. Why are they doing this? Does it matter? Why? Why not?

📖 Read to the point of the story in which Horace and Sylvester decide to race each other and fall into a deep hole.

🛑 Why does Horace dare Sylvester to race? Will this settle the argument? Why? Why not? What is the problem now? Ask for a variety of solutions. Older students can even generate consequences.

📖 Read to the point of the story in which the two friends are free again.

🛑 Does boasting help get them out? How do they feel about being free again?

📖 Finish the story.

🛑 How are they perfect in different ways? Why is Horace grateful? Why do they meet under the old baobab tree? Who wins the battle? Why? What was good about working together?

After Reading

What values do students recognize in this story? What other stories are similar to this one? How are they different? What real-life incidents touch on the same issue?

Friendship
Giving
Perseverance
Self-Discipline
Compassion
Responsibility
Respect
Honesty

The Big Boasting Battle
Extension Activities

Character Qualities

Create a chart listing the strengths of Horace and Sylvester. Draw lines connecting strengths that are similar. Ask students to draw a picture of each character. Then ask them to write a description of the character in a circle around the character.

Lions and Snakes

Provide a room full of lions and snakes. To make snakes, stuff one leg of panty hose with newspaper. Add eyes, a nose and mouth to give the snake(s) personality.

Use a large piece of tan construction paper for the body of the lion. Cut off the corners to round them. Add a brown rope and brown pom-pom for the tail. Make the head out of a paper plate. Add tan or brown yarn, doll hair or dried grass around the plate for the mane. Glue on eyes, a nose, ears and a mouth.

Journal Entry

Ask students to write about one of their own personality strengths and weaknesses. Ask them to describe each trait and explain how it helps or hinders them.

How Big Is Big?

Discuss *exaggeration*. Give children a piece of paper, and ask them to draw a picture of something from the story that is big. Give them additional pieces of paper to draw bigger and bigger things. Pair students and ask them to describe one of the objects to another student. They must try to pick out the specific object that is being described.

Related Readings

Try reading *Wolf's Chicken Stew* (Keiko).

Honesty   Respect   Responsibility   Compassion   Self-Discipline   Perseverance   Giving   Friendship

Frederick
Storing Memories

Summary

All the mice worked hard to store supplies for the winter, except Frederick. Frederick gathered colors and words instead. When the food supplies ran out, it was Frederick who painted pictures with his words and kept the mice entertained.

Before Reading

Have students remember a summer day by closing their eyes and imagining the colors, sounds and sights. Ask them to share their images with the class.

While Reading

📖 Read to the part of the story in which the mice are working so hard to store supplies.

🛑 What kinds of things do the mice gather? What does Frederick gather? How do the students feel about gathering supplies while Frederick isn't doing his share of the work? What should the mice do? How might Frederick react?

📖 Read to the point of the story in which Frederick stores something besides food.

🛑 What images does Frederick share? How do these images make the other mice feel?

After Reading

Read several poems with bright colors and vivid images to the children. Discuss why people like poetry. What values do students recognize in this story? What other stories are similar to this one? How are they different? What real-life incidents touch on the same issues?

Frederick
Extension Activities

Art Activity

Make a collage of colors for each of the seasons. Ask students to bring in pieces of paper, greeting cards and fabric that show the colors, sights and sounds of the season.

Dramatic Play

Make mouse masks with paper plates to act out the story of Frederick. Cut out the eyes, nose and mouth from the center of the paper plate and attach a tongue depressor as a handle. Color the masks to look like mice. Attach construction paper ears to the masks.

Special Treasures

Ask students to share the story of Frederick with their family and then interview family members to find out one thing each would choose to take into a cave for the winter. Compile the interviews into a class list to compare results. Some ideas will be practical and some will be creative like Frederick's colors and words.

Related Readings

Read other books by Leo Lionni to compare illustrations and characters: *Fish Is Fish* and *Alexander and the Wind-Up Mouse*.

I Hate My Brother Harry
Sibling Rivalry

Summary

Harry's little sister says she hates her brother. He is sometimes nice to her, but the teasing never stops.

Before Reading

How old are the children on the cover? Look at the girl's face. How does she feel? Discuss the title and show her drawing on the title page.

While Reading

📖 Read to the part of the story in which Harry tells his sister he put chopped-up frogs in the frosting.

🛑 Why does Harry tell his sister he put chopped-up frogs in the brownies frosting? How does she feel? Why is he telling her this?

📖 Read to the point of the story in which the sister says that someday she will spit in her brother's pudding.

🛑 Why does she say this? What could she do instead?

📖 Finish the story.

🛑 Why does she say hateful things back to Harry? What could she do instead? Does she really mean the things she says? Ask the children if they have ever said hateful things to their brother/sister/others? What are other alternatives?

After Reading

What values do students recognize in this story? What other stories are similar to this one? How are they different? What real-life incidents touch on the same issues?

Friendship Giving Perseverance Self-Discipline Compassion Responsibility Respect Honesty

I Hate My Brother Harry
Extension Activities

Mean Harry and Nice Harry

On the chalkboard or chart paper, make two columns. Label the columns *Mean Harry* and *Nice Harry*. Ask the students to recall things that happened in the story, and write them in the corresponding columns. Students' ideas will probably differ.

Make Frog Frosting

Make enough brownies so each student will have one. Have a few extra. Making the brownies could be a class activity. Prepare or buy a large amount of plain frosting. Add extra milk to make the frosting easier to spread. Provide a variety of food coloring for the students to choose from. Individually, or in small groups, give each student frosting in a small container. Allow students to mix food coloring to make the "frog" frosting of their choice. Then they may spread the frosting on the brownie. Serve milk.

Class Big Book

Give each student drawing paper with this printed on the bottom: *I don't like to be teased about . . .* Ask each student to finish the sentence and illustrate their answer. Assemble the pages into a class big book with a cover that looks like a brownie with "frog" frosting. The title on the cover should look like it is written with frosting.

Inch by Inch
Being Useful

Summary

An inchworm tries to show his usefulness by measuring many things. Then the nightingale threatens to eat him if he doesn't measure her song. The story shows how he outsmarts the nightingale.

Before Reading

Find the inchworm on the cover. Why is he called an inchworm? Show an inch on a ruler. Find the inchworm on the title page.

While Reading

📖 Read about the robin on the first page.

🛑 Find the inchworm. What are some things the robin might do?

📖 Read to the point of the story in which the nightingale asks the inchworm to measure her song.

🛑 Can he measure the song? How can a song be measured? What is his idea?

📖 Read to the point of the story in which the nightingale signs and the inchworm measures. Read up to the last page.

🛑 Where is the inchworm on each page? What is he doing?

📖 Finish the story.

🛑 How does the inchworm solve the problem? Is it right for the nightingale to want to eat the inchworm? Why or why not? Answers to these questions will vary. What other ways do animals escape from each other?

After Reading

What values do students recognize in this story? What other stories are similar to this one? How are they different? What real-life incidents touch on the same issue?

Friendship Giving Perseverance Self-Discipline Compassion Responsibility Respect Honesty

Inch by Inch
Extension Activities

Inchworm Rulers

Use the 6" (15 cm) ruler design to make several ruler copies out of heavy paper for students. Cut different colored stripes of construction paper approximately 2" x 12" (5 x 30 cm). Each student should glue two of the 6" (15 cm) rulers onto the 12" (30 cm) strip to make a 12" (30 cm) ruler. Students should make the head of the inchworm at one end and a tail at the other end. They may also add an eye and their name to the inchworm.

Measuring with the Inchworm Ruler

Using the inchworm rulers, measure each animal part in the illustrations throughout the story. Record all the measurements on a chart. Find other things in the room that are the same length.

Animal	Inches	Other Objects
robin's tail		
flamingo's neck		
toucan's beak		
heron's leg		
pheasant's tail		
hummingbird		

Measurement Center

Prepare a measuring center. Put objects that are less than 12" (30 cm) in length in the center. Use pencils of various sizes, blocks, crayons, empty milk cartons, books, shoe, mittens, etc. Students should practice measuring each item. Some of the students will realize that some items have more than one side to measure. Some students will also realize the need for a 1/2" (1.25 cm) measurement.

Story Alternatives

Use many colors of construction paper, wallpaper scraps, felt or other art supplies to make inchworms. Students can help make flowers, leaves and reeds to add to a wall-sized mural. Refer the students to the last two pages of the story to see how the author describes the mural. Glue items to the mural to create a 3-D effect.

Honesty Respect Responsibility Compassion Self-Discipline Perseverance Giving Friendship

The Quarreling Book
It Takes Everyone to Get Along

Summary

It is a rainy, gray day when Mr. James forgets to kiss his wife good-bye. That hurts Mrs. James' feelings, so she is cross with Johnathon. He takes it out on Sally. One character after another shares the grumpiness until the dog turns things around. The day turns out happy after all.

Before Reading

Ask students to discuss how they feel when someone isn't nice to them.

While Reading

📖 Read to the part of the story in which Marjorie calls her little brother a sissy.

🛑 Why does Marjorie call Eddie a sissy? How does this make Eddie feel? What could Marjorie have done instead?

📖 Read to the point of the story in which Eddie shoves the dog off the bed.

🛑 Should Eddie be angry with the dog? What other things could he have done to show his anger? What will the dog do next? How will everyone feel?

📖 Read to the point of the story in which Mr. James arrives home and kisses Mrs. James hello.

🛑 Marjorie tells Eddie she is sorry she called him a sissy. Sally says she is sorry she made Marjorie feel bad. Why do the characters forgive each other? What would have happened if the dog hadn't wanted to play? What does it mean to apologize? Ask students what they do when someone apologizes to them?

After Reading

What values do students recognize in this story? What other stories are similar to this one? How are they different? What real-life incidents touch on the same issue?

Honesty Respect Responsibility Compassion Self-Discipline Perseverance Giving Friendship

The Quarreling Book
Extension Activities

Happy and Sad

Draw a happy face on one side of a paper plate and a sad face on the other side. Attach a tongue depressor for a handle.

Retell the story. Ask students to hold up the appropriate face to show how the characters act in the story.

Illustration

Find a picture on a page in this book that shows this book was written and illustrated a long time ago. Draw a new picture for that page to make it look like the present.

Related Readings

Zolotow has written many books about feelings. *The Hating Book* (1969) deals with friendship.

Smoky Night
Neighborliness

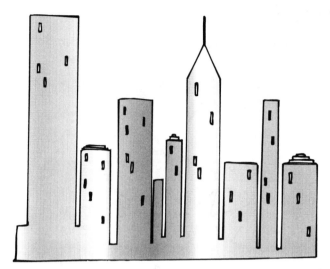

Summary

This 1995 Caldecott award winner tells the story of the Los Angeles riots. Two cats teach people how to get along. It shows how people are brought together regardless of their cultural diversity.

Before Reading

Make predictions by looking at the cover and discussing the title. Discuss the artwork on the end pages. Point out the author's dedication. Predict what it means.

While Reading

📖 Read to the part of the story in which the street becomes empty after Daniel and Mama watch the looting.

🛑 Why are people stealing things that belong to others? Ask students how they feel when someone takes something that belongs to them? Why doesn't the family shop at Mr. Kim's store?

📖 Read to the point of the story in which everyone leaves the building while the railing is too hot to touch.

🛑 What causes the fire? Who starts the fire? How does everyone leaving the building feel?

📖 Finish the story.

🛑 How do the cats bring the neighbors together and make them friends? What is the meaning of the author's dedication? How do people help each other in this story? What happens when people take what doesn't belong to them? Ask how the students would feel if someone would take something of theirs or set fire to their home? How do others feel if their property is stolen or damaged? Ask students to tell about something the people in their neighborhood do to help each other.

After Reading

What values do students recognize in this story? What other stories are similar to this one? How are they different? What real-life incidents touch on the same issues?

Friendship Giving Perseverance Self-Discipline Compassion Responsibility Respect Honesty

Smoky Night
Extension Activities

Friends: Alike and Different

Divide the group into partners. Ask each student to choose the animal they would like to be. The animals may be of the same species or maybe other animals who are not usually friends. Use the following ideas, and role-play each situation. Students can practice and each pair should select one role to perform to the whole group.

- How are the two animals different?

- How are the two animals alike?

- Why don't the two animals like each other?

- Ask one another to be friends.

- Invite the other to spend the day together. What would the animals do together?

Collage

Return to the story and spend time observing and commenting on David Diaz's collage technique. Provide a collection of different materials for students to create their own collage. Some of the materials may include: construction paper scraps, buttons, seeds, marconi, rice, wood bark, sand, oatmeal, crushed eggshells, dry tempera, birdseed, newspaper, tissue paper, brown paper bags, tissues, shredded decorative grass, packing baubles, etc.

Media Watch: Acts of Kindness

Watch print and video news for similar situations. Older students can bring articles from the newspaper and magazines as well as report the television or radio news. Use the events for follow-up discussions. Post the articles on a bulletin board.

Stellaluna
Different but Alike

Summary

Separated from her mother, a baby bat named Stellaluna is adopted by a bird family. She learns how to be a bird. Stellaluna is finally reunited with her real mother, but her friendship with the bird family remains.

Before Reading

Read the Bat Notes at the end of this book. Discuss the habits of bats. Do bats really fly? What do bats eat? Where do they live? Should people be afraid of bats? How do bats help people?

While Reading

Read to the part of the story in which Stellaluna is separated from her mother.

STOP Discuss ways in which bats are similar to birds. What will the birds' reaction be to Stellaluna? What should the birds do? What should Stellaluna do?

Read to the point of the story in which Mama Bird orders Stellaluna to obey her rules.

STOP What habits does Stellaluna learn from the birds? Why is Mama Bird so upset with Stellaluna when she teaches the birds to hang upside down? Do different people have different rules? What rules do children have that adults don't have? What rules do adults have that children don't have?

Finish the story. Reread the section in which they discover how alike and how different they are.

STOP Discuss ways people can be very different yet be good friends. What would happen if everyone were alike? How can being different make a person special to others?

After Reading

What values do students recognize in this story? What other stories are similar to this one? How are they different? What real-life incidents touch on the same issues?

Friendship   Giving   Perseverance   Self-Discipline   Compassion   Responsibility   Respect   Honesty

39

Stellaluna
Extension Activities

Bat Trivia

Bring books about bats to class so students can collect bat trivia. Create bat shapes on card stock. Record bat trivia on the bat cards and post each piece of information on a bulletin board.

We Are All Alike
We Are All Different

Put students in pairs. Ask them to draw a picture of themselves on each half of a folded sheet of paper.

As they look at the picture, ask them to tell each other how they are alike and how they are different. (Both might have brown eyes, but one may be blonde while the other has black hair, etc.) Older students may list similarities and differences. Use the recording sheet on page 41.

Dramatic Play

Divide the class into groups. Ask each group to act out a scene in *Stellaluna*. Some suggested scenes are: when Stellaluna learns to eat bugs, when Stellaluna teaches the bird to land upside down and when Stellaluna tells the other bats the things she has been learning.

Related Readings

For other stories that might be similar, try *Are You My Mother?* by Philip D. Eastman.

Left margin (bottom to top): Honesty Respect Responsibility Compassion Self-Discipline Perseverance Giving Friendship

We Are All Alike

_____

_____

_____

_____

_____

_____

_____

_____

_____

_____

_____

_____

_____

_____

_____

_____

_____

_____

_____

_____

We Are All Different

_____

_____

_____

_____

_____

_____

_____

_____

_____

_____

_____

_____

_____

_____

_____

_____

_____

_____

_____

_____

Honesty   Respect   Responsibility   Compassion   Self-Discipline   Perseverance   Giving   Friendship

41

Bibliography

Bunting, Eve. (1994). *Smoky Night.* Ill. David Diaz. New York: Harcourt Brace & Company. ISBN: 0-15-269954-6

Cannon, Janell. (1993). *Stellaluna.* New York: Harcourt Brace & Company. ISBN: 0-15-280217-7

Dragonwagon, Crescent. (1983). *I Hate My Brother Harry.* Ill. Dick Gackenbach. New York: Harper & Row. ISBN: 0-440-84145-3

Eastman, P.D. (1960). *Are You My Mother?* New York: Random House. ISBN: 0-394-80018-4

Eastman, P.D. (1967). *¿Eres tu mi mama?* New York: Random House. ISBN: 0-679-84330-2

Eastman, P.D. (1986). *Are You My Mother?* (audiocassette). New York: Random House.

Eastman, P.D. (1991). *Are You My Mother?* (videocassette). New York: Random House Video.

Keiko. (1989). *Wolf's Chicken Stew.* New York: Putnam Publishing Group. ISBN: 0-399-22000-3

Lionni, Leo. (1974). *Alexander and the Wind-Up Mouse.* New York: Knopf/Pantheon.

Lionni, Leo. (1967). *Frederick.* New York: Knopf Books. ISBN: 0-394-82614-0

Lionni, Leo. (1976). *Frederick and Ten Other Stories.* (audiocassette). Caedmon.

Lionni, Leo. (1970). *Fish Is Fish.* New York: Pantheon Books. ISBN: 0-394-90440-0

Lionni, Leo. (1987). *Five Lionni Classics.* (videocassette). Italtoons Corporation: A Giulio Gianini/Leo Lionni Production. Random House Home Video. (Closed captioned)

Lionni, Leo. (1960). *Inch by Inch.* New York: Scholastic Inc. ISBN: 0-590-47991-1

Lionni, Leo. (1985). *Leo Lionni's Caldecotts.* (videocassette). Random House/Miller Brody Production.

Wilhelm, Hans. (1995). *The Big Boasting Battle.* New York: Scholastic Inc. ISBN: 0-590-22211-2

Zolotow, Charlotte. (1969). *The Hating Book.* New York: Harper & Row. ISBN: 0-06-026924-3

Zolotow, Charlotte. (1963). *The Quarreling Book.* Ill. by Arnold Lobel. New York: HarperCollins. ISBN: 0-06-443034-0

Dear Parents,

This week we are studying about *responsibility,* one of the virtues that Dr. Ernest Boyer suggests schools should examine. Dr. Boyer defines *responsibility* as "Each person has a sense of duty to fulfill willingly the tasks he or she has accepted or has been assigned. All work is conscientiously performed. Members of the community feel comfortable asking for help and agree that they must be held accountable for their behavior." Ernest Boyer, before his death late in 1995, served as U.S. Commissioner of Education and was president of The Carnegie Foundation for the Advancement of Teaching.

Several books for young children address *responsibility.* These books include:

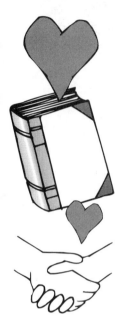

Another Mouse to Feed
Five Minutes Peace
Herbie's Troubles
Luke's Bully
Mother's Day Mice
Sachiko Means Happiness
The Song and Dance Man
Strega Nona
Swimmy
Tell Me a Mitzi
Wilfrid Gordon McDonald Partridge

We will read some of these in class.

Expect your child/children to use terms like *duty, complete, accountable* and *conscientious* in their conversations with you this week. You may have an opportunity to share your feelings with your child/children about *responsibility.* Please feel free to call me with questions and concerns.

Sincerely,

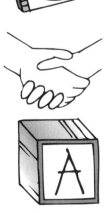

43

Another Mouse to Feed
Responsible Children Help Out

Summary

Mr. and Mrs. Mouse have many children. It is difficult for them to take care of their large family. One day someone leaves baby mouse on their front doorstep. The children help their parents solve the problems.

While Reading

Read to the part of the story in which Mrs. Mouse gets a job and Mr. Mouse has three jobs.

STOP Why are Mr. and Mrs. Mouse so tired? How does being tired make them feel towards their family? What consequences would the family feel if Mrs. Mouse doesn't get a job outside the home and Mr. Mouse only has one job?

Read to the point of the story in which the baby is found on the doorstep.

STOP Pause for the children to view the picture and think about the message. Who put the baby on the doorstep? Why would someone do that? How do Mr. and Mrs. Mouse feel when they say, "A mouse in need is another mouse to feed?" Mrs. Mouse starts the sentence but Mr. Mouse finishes it. How would she have finished the sentence? Why? What will the family do?

Finish the story as the mouse children help out.

STOP Ask students how they can help their families like the mouse children help their parents. Why should every family member help?

After Reading

What values do students recognize in this story? What other stories are similar to this one? How are they different? What real-life incidents touch on the same issue?

Another Mouse to Feed
Extension Activities

How Many Mouths to Feed?

Count the mouse children on the beginning text pages of the story. Compare the size of the mouse family with the size of students' families.

Place the number of mouse children on a cheese-shaped piece of paper. Attach it to a class graph. Place the number of people in each child's family on a piece of cheese. Attach it to the graph.

Older children can plan a meal for themselves, and then try to figure out how much food it takes to feed the class or the mouse family.

Which Job for Me?

List Mr. Mouse's three jobs. Provide props (brooms, mops, dusters) in the dramatic play area for children to practice job skills. Work with older children to generate a list of parents' jobs at home and at work.

Where Does All the Money Go?

Provide each student with a piece of paper folded into several boxes. Ask students to draw something their family spends money on each box. Label and cut out each box. Glue the boxes onto a piece of paper folded in half and labeled *Necessities* and *Extras*. Use this book as a introduction to a money unit emphasizing Edgar's role of taking care of the money.

Everyone Helps

Create a class book, *Everyone Helps*. Each student should draw and/or write about how they help at home. Assemble the pages into a class book.

Herbie's Troubles
Bullies

Summary

Herbie has troubles with a boy at school named Jimmy John. Jimmy John causes so many troubles that Herbie doesn't want to go to school anymore. Other friends have solutions but none of them work. Herbie has to solve the problem all by himself.

Before Reading

Discuss the pictures on the cover. Then read the title. Make some predictions about what Herbie's troubles might be.

While Reading

Read to the part of the story in which Herbie doesn't want to go to school anymore.

STOP Why doesn't Herbie want to go to school anymore?

Read to the point of the story in which Sophie's suggestion doesn't work.

STOP What does Sophie mean when she says, "Be assertive?" How is Herbie assertive? Does it work? Are there better solutions?

Read to the point of the story in which Herbie tries Jake's idea.

STOP What is Jake's solution? Does it solve the problem? Does it match one of the solutions students offered? What alternative solutions are left?

Finish the story.

STOP Does Herbie decide he does not want to stay home from school? How does he solve the problem with Jimmy John? Is it like one of the solutions students offered?

After Reading

What values do students recognize in this story? What other stories are similar to this one? How are they different? What real-life incidents touch on the same issues?

Herbie's Troubles
Extension Activities

Sharing

As a whole group or in small groups, ask students to share about a time when they solved a problem with a friend, brother or sister. Encourage students to ask each other about the way the problem was solved.

Story Map

Retell the story. Ask students to identify the problems. Record the problems on sentence strips. Ask the students to identify events leading toward the solution. Record the events on sentence strips that are a different color than the problem strips. Ask the students to identify the solution. Record the solution on a sentence strip that is a different color than the problem and events strips. Ask the students about the relationship between the problem and the solution. If different color sentence strips are not available, use different color markers for each of the three categories. Using three colors will help students understand the problems, events and solution relationship. Reproducibles are provided at the end of this book for this activity.

Pair Up for Problem Solving

Make a list of the problems that have occurred in the classroom recently. Include times and places, such as on the playground, on the bus and in the lunchroom. Write each problem on a card. Pair the students. Give each pair one of the problem cards. Tell younger students the problem on the card. Older students can read it themselves. Ask each pair to decide on a solution to the problem. They may dramatize the problem and solution or explain it. Ask for additional suggestions from the group.

Related Readings

Another related book is *Luke's Bully* by Elizabeth Winthrop.

Mitzi Sneezes from Tell Me a Mitzi
Taking Care of Each Other

Summary

Jacob and Mitzi both come down with a bad cold. Their mother brings them hot soup and orange juice and takes care of them. Then their father comes home from work with a bad cold. Their mother has three sick patients to care for. Their mother also catches the cold, so Grandmother has to take care of them all. Finally they get well, but Grandmother catches their cold. Everyone pitches in to take care of Grandmother because it is her turn to be the patient.

Before Reading

Discuss how to care for someone who is sick. Ask students who takes care of them when they are sick? How would they help take care of someone in their family who is sick?

While Reading

Read to the part of the story in which Mitzi and Jacob's mother discovers Jacob is sick.

STOP How does Mother know that Jacob is sick? Ask students how they feel when they have a bad cold? What could they do?

Read to the point of the story in which Mitzi, Jacob, Mother and Father are all feeling better.

STOP List the things Mitzi's grandmother does to help them all feel better. Which of these things were listed when students thought of things Mitzi and Jacob's mother could do?

Finish the story.

STOP Why does Mitzi's grandmother say it is the best cold she has ever had? Ask students how people take care of them when they are sick?

After Reading

What values do students recognize in this story? What other stories are similar to this one? How are they different? What real-life incidents touch on the same issue?

48

Mitzi Sneezes
Extension Activities

Healthy Foods

Mitzi's mother brings food on a tray. Ask the children to draw a picture of a tray of foods they like to eat when they have a bad cold. Ask them to label each food on the tray and draw a flower on the tray to cheer up the sick patient.

Storytelling

Mitzi and Jacob like to hear stories when they are sick. Help Mitzi and Jacob finish this story by filling in the blanks. Illustrate the story on the back of the page.

Once upon a time there was a _____

named _____ with a bad cold.

The cold made _____ very grumpy.

Father and Mother tried to cheer up their little _____

by _____.

But the _____ only felt worse.

Finally, Father decided to bring a glass of _____

to the little _____. That made

_____ feel much better.

Then Mother got out _____, _____'s favorite game.

Soon _____ was well enough to go out and play.

Honesty   Respect   **Responsibility**   Compassion   Self-Discipline   Perseverance   Giving   Friendship

Sachiko Means Happiness
Respect Comes from Responsibility and Understanding

Summary

Each evening Sachiko is asked to talk with her grand-mother (whose name is also Sachiko) while her mother fixes dinner. Because of Alzheimers, Grandmother has changed in the past few years from the loving person who gave Sachiko special attention, to someone who scarcely recognizes her. Each evening with dread, Sachiko talks with her grandmother. One evening Sachiko realizes that her grandmother is afraid, and offers in a child-like way, to spend the night with her. They walk to dinner as friends.

Before Reading

The author shares memories of her grandmother in *Note from the Author* at the back of the book. Here she tells children how Alzheimers changed her grandmother. Sharing this information before or after reading the story might change the decisions students make at the stopping points in the story.

While Reading

📖 Read to the part of the story in which Mother first asks Sachiko to talk with Grandmother.

🛑 Why does Mother need Sachiko to talk with Grandmother? What will they talk about?

📖 Read to the point of the story in which Sachiko asks herself why she has to take care of her grandmother.

🛑 If Sachiko doesn't want to take care of Grandmother, what should she do? What will happen if she does take care of her? If she doesn't?

📖 Read to the point of the story in which Sachiko realizes that it must be difficult to discover that everyone is a stranger.

🛑 What will Sachiko do now? Why?

📖 Finish the story.

🛑 How does Sachiko show respect and compassion for her grandmother?

After Reading

What values do students recognize in this story? What other stories are similar to this one? How are they different? What real-life incidents touch on the same issues?

Sachiko Means Happiness
Extension Activities

Letters to Grandparents

Ask parents to send an addressed and stamped envelope(s) to school so children can "write" and mail a letter to their grandparent(s).

Provide students with stationery. Ask them to write or draw a picture to send to their grandparents. Have a few names of folks in the local nursing home for students who do not have grandparents.

Where in the World?

Provide a map so students can find their grandparents' home. Place a pin on the spot to mark each grandparent. Connect the spots with yarn. Mark each pin with the appropriate child's name.

Times with Grandma

Ask each student to draw a picture or write a paragraph about how they like to spend time with their grandmother. Note what each student says on the back of their picture. Make a class book of *Times with Grandmother*.

Repeat the activity for Grandfather.

Field Trip

Ask students to write stories, paint pictures and copy poems. Frame each creation with paper in the colors of the season. Visit a nursing home with students so they may deliver their gifts.

Honesty Respect Responsibility Compassion Self-Discipline Perseverance Giving Friendship

Strega Nona
A Pot of Trouble!

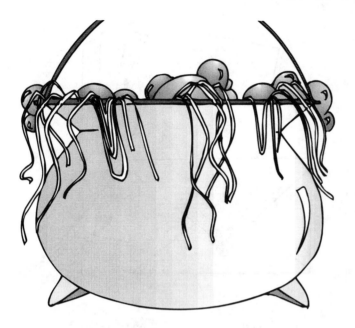

Summary

Strega Nona hired Big Anthony to help her but told him he must never touch the pasta pot. When Strega Nona left Big Anthony in charge, he decided to try her magic spell. But he didn't know how to turn the spell off, so pasta kept pouring out of the magic pot! Strega Nona returned just in time to save Big Anthony from the angry townspeople and stop the pasta from burying the town. Big Anthony learned his lesson. He ended up eating all the extra pasta.

Before Reading

Discuss the responsibilities that come with a job. What happens when someone does not do their job well? Also discuss the importance of following directions carefully.

While Reading

Read to the part of the story in which Big Anthony discovers the magic spell.

Discuss why Strega Nona wants to keep her magic spell a secret. What could happen if someone discovers the magic spell? What will Big Anthony do? What could happen if he does?

Read to the point of the story in which Big Anthony uses the magic spell and finds out what happens?

Why does Big Anthony want to try the magic spell? What should he do when he does find out? How does Big Anthony feel when the townspeople cheer him?

Finish the story.

What punishment does Strega Nona give Big Anthony? What lesson does Big Anthony learn?

After Reading

What values do students recognize in this story? What other stories are similar to this one? How are they different? What real-life incidents touch on the same issues?

Strega Nona
Extension Activities

Pasta, Pasta, Everywhere!

String necklaces with pasta to wear on pasta day. Then assign jobs to make spaghetti or macaroni. Discuss the importance of each task being carried out carefully. Task badges are provided on page 54.

Fill the pot with water.
Heat the water.
Time the pasta cooking.
Drain the pasta.
Heat the pasta sauce.

Mix the pasta and sauce.
Set the table.
Serve the pasta and sauce.
Clean up the pots and pans.
Clean off the tables. Throw away trash.

Readers' Theater

Use this story for a Readers' Theater presentation. Develop some of the townspeople's parts, using simple and short lines. Present the skit to another class or to parents.

Magic Spells

Ask the students to write their own magic spells for cooking different foods. For example, a magic spell to cook pizza or ice cream.

Pasta Sorting and Tasting

Buy various types of pasta and put them in a bowl. Ask students to sort the pastas by shape into different colored bowls.

Boil various types of pasta and return them to the bowls. Allow students to take a few to taste. Use several different types of sauces.

Friendship Giving Perseverance Self-Discipline Compassion Responsibility Respect Honesty

Fill the pot with water.	Heat the water.	Time the pasta cooking.
Drain the pasta.	Heat the pasta sauce.	Mix the pasta and sauce.
Set the table.	Serve the pasta and sauce.	Clean up the pots and pans.
Clean off the tables.	Throw away trash.	

Task Badges

Swimmy

Working together as a team makes things better for everyone.

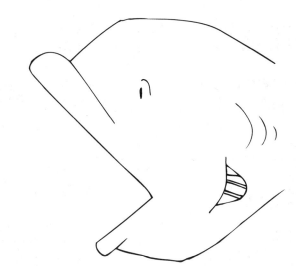

Summary

Swimmy escapes when a big tuna fish swallows all the other fish in the school. He enjoys swimming around and becoming acquainted with all the wonderful creatures in the sea. Then one day Swimmy meets a school of fish hiding in the rocks. They are afraid the big fish will eat them. Swimmy teaches them to use teamwork to solve the problem.

While Reading

Read to the part of the story in which Swimmy escapes when the big tuna eats the red fish.

STOP Why is Swimmy able to escape? What will happen next? What problems are ahead for Swimmy?

Read to the point of the story in which Swimmy sees sea anemones that look like pink palm trees swaying in the wind.

STOP Verify the students' predictions. What does happen? Does it match any of the class's predictions? What problem(s) confront Swimmy? What does he do when he meets a problem? Is he happy or sad? Why does he feel this way?

Read to the point of the story in which Swimmy tells the new school of fish they can't just lie there.

STOP Why does Swimmy tell the new school of fish to think of solutions? What is the problem? What ideas will solve the problem? What could happen with each idea?

Finish the story.

STOP What is the plan? Does it fool the big fish? Why does the plan chase the big fish away? How do Swimmy and the red fish solve the problem?

After Reading

What values do students recognize in this story? What other stories are similar to this one? How are they different? What real-life incidents touch on the same issues?

Swimmy
Extension Activities

Red Fish in the Sea

Examine the book's illustrations. Use pieces of sponge dipped in paint to make a wall mural of the red fish in the shape of a large fish with Swimmy as the eye. Seaweed and other underwater plants and animals can be added.

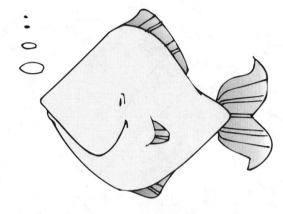

What Happens Next?

Ask students to write a continuation of the story telling how Swimmy and the school of red fish continue to live in the ocean. Young children may tell the story in pictures. A small fish sponge and red paint will help them "draw" the small fish (see the above activity). Older children may write on story-book paper to make a set of stories into a chapter book.

How Many Little Fish Does It Take?

Draw a fish large enough to fill a half page. Ask students to put fish crackers on the fish, all facing the same direction. Fit as many as possible on the large fish. Count how many little fish it takes to make the large fish, and record the number on a class graph. Enjoy a fish snack of crackers.

Related Readings

Read *Amos and Boris* (William Steig).

Bibliography

Ackerman, Karen. (1988). *The Song and Dance Man*. New York: Knopf, Inc. ISBN: 0-394-89330-1

Bunting, Eve. (1986). *Mother's Day Mice*. Ill. Jan Brett. New York: Clarion. ISBN: 0-89919-702-7

Chapman, Carol. (1981). *Herbie's Troubles*. Ill. Kelly Oechsli. New York: Dutton Publishing Co., Inc. ISBN: 0-525-31645-0

De Paola, Tomie. (1975). *Strega Nona*. New York: Simon & Schuster. ISBN: 0671-66606-1

Fox, Mem. (1993). *Wilfrid Gordon McDonald Partridge*. Kane/Miller. ISBN: 0-916291-26-X

Kraus, Robert. (1980). Ill. Jose Aruego and Ariane Dewey. *Another Mouse to Feed*. New York: Simon & Schuster. ISBN: 0-440-84548-3

Lionni, Leo. (1963). *Swimmy*. New York: Alfred A. Knopf, Inc. ISBN: 0-590-43049-1

Murphy, Jill. (1986). *Five Minutes Peace*. New York: G.P. Putnam's Sons. ISBN: 0-399-21354-6

Sakai, Kimiko. (1990). *Sachiko Means Happiness*. San Francisco: Children's Book Press. ISBN: 0-89239-065-4

Segal, Lore. (1991). *Tell Me a Mitzi*. New York: Farrar, Strauss and Giroux. ISBN: 0-374-47502-4

Steig, William. (1992). *Amos and Boris*. New York: Farrar, Strauss, and Giroux. ISBN: 0-374-30279-0

Winthrop, E. (1990). *Luke's Bully*. New York: Viking.

Honesty   Respect   Responsibility   Compassion   Self-Discipline   Perseverance   Giving   Friendship

Dear Parents,

This week we are studying about *compassion,* one of the virtues that Dr. Ernest Boyer suggests schools should examine. Dr. Boyer defines *compassion* as "Each person is considerate and caring. There is a recognition that everyone, from time to time, feels hurt, confused, angry, or sad. Instead of ignoring such conditions, people reach out to one another. In the case of conflict, members of the community seek reconciliation and try to understand each other, even forgive." Ernest Boyer, before his death late in 1995, served as U.S. Commissioner of Education and was president of The Carnegie Foundation for the Advancement of Teaching.

Several books for young children address *compassion.* These books include:

Alexander and the Terrible, Horrible, No Good, Very Bad Day
Amelia Bedelia books
Angel Child, Dragon Child
Big Al
The Big Orange Splot
Crow Boy
Dribbles
Jamaica Tag-Along
The King Who Rained
Little Monster at School
Mean Soup
Owl Moon
Rainbow Fish
Swimmy

We will read some of these in class.

Expect your child/children to use terms like *considerate, caring, compassion, reconciliation* and *forgiveness* in their conversations with you this week. You may have an opportunity to share your feelings with your child/children about *compassion.* Please feel free to call me with questions and concerns.

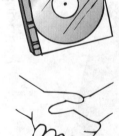

Sincerely,

58

Big Al
Being a Friend Doesn't Mean Being the Same

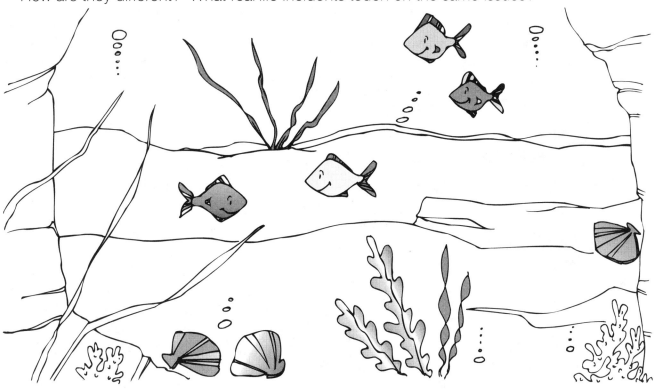

Summary

Big Al is a big, scary-looking fish who has no friends. He tries many things to make friends with the other fish. All the fish learn that each one looks different but that different is special.

While Reading

📖 Read to the part of the story in which Big Al watches the net drop from above.

🛑 How does Big Al feel as he sees all the fish caught in the net? What are the smaller fish thinking? What could the little fish do? What could Big Al do?

📖 Finish the story.

🛑 How can the little fish help Big Al? How can Big Al help the little fish? Ask students how many of these solutions they thought of themselves.

After Reading

What values do students recognize in this story? What other stories are similar to this one? How are they different? What real-life incidents touch on the same issues?

Friendship · Giving · Perseverance · Self-Discipline · Compassion · Responsibility · Respect · Honesty

Friendship
Giving
Perseverance
Self-Discipline
Compassion
Responsibility
Respect
Honesty

Big Al
Extension Activities

Catch Big Fish and Little Fish

Cut an inexpensive fish net into pieces so that each student has two pieces. Glue it on three sides to pieces of paper the same shape. Place scraps of construction paper of different colors on the table with fish-shaped stencils. Ask students to trace around the stencils, cut out the little fish and put them into the fish net. Allow students to put the small fish on an overhead, and project them onto a bulletin board which has a piece of paper taped to it. Older students can add adjectives to each fish in the net to describe the little fish. They may write adjectives on the large fish to describe Big Al.

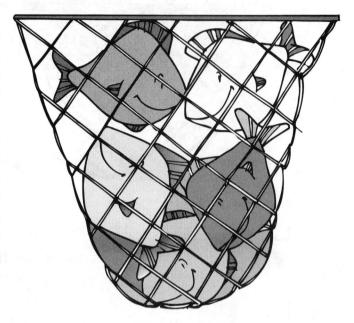

Big Al

Cut large fish shapes to make a *Big Al Big Book.* Ask each student to draw a picture or write stories about Big Al helping the little fish. Put the stories together in the book.

All Together in the Ocean

Cut a piece of white butcher paper the size of a bulletin board. Ask students to paint it with light blue paint. Let it dry. Put it on the bulletin board.

Provide fish stencils or paper scissors for students to paint the little fish that play with Big Al, after the fish learn that he is a friend. Big Al can be a class project, with each student painting one part. Glue on googlie eyes to make Big Al's portrait stand out.

Older students can write about what the little fish could do with Big Al.

The Big Orange Splot
It's Okay Being Different

Summary

Mr. Plumbean lives on a street where all the houses are alike. After a seagull drops a can of orange paint on Mr. Plumbean's house, he paints his house. He paints his house to match his dreams. At first his neighbors are unhappy but gradually begin changing their houses to fit their dreams. The street is no longer neat, but shows their dreams.

While Reading

📖 Read to the part of the story in which the orange paint can drops on Mr. Plumbean's house.

🛑 Turn back to the front cover. Show that the can of dropped paint caused "The Big Orange Splot." What problems could this cause? How does he feel? How do the neighbors feel? What will he do? What will they do?

📖 Continue reading as Mr. Plumbean decides to paint his house with elephants, lions, pretty girls and steam shovels.

🛑 The neighbors want him to paint his house to cover the big orange splot. Are they happy to have this house on their street? Why? Why not? Ask students if all the houses on their street are the same.

📖 Read to the point of the story in which the next-door neighbor paints his house to look like a ship.

🛑 Why does the neighbor paint his house to look like a ship? What will the other neighbors say? Why? Ask students what they would say. Why?

📖 Finish the story.

🛑 Why does each neighbor change his house? Ask students what they would do with their houses?

After Reading

What values do students recognize in this story? What other stories are similar to this one? How are they different? What real-life incidents touch on the same issue?

Honesty   Respect   Responsibility   **Compassion**   Self-Discipline   Perseverance   Giving   Friendship

The Big Orange Splot
Extension Activities

Dream House

Provide each child with white sacks of various sizes, construction paper, markers and glue. Ask them to color the front of the house on one side of the white sack and the back of the house on the other side of the sack. Stuff the sacks with newspaper, and decorate a piece of construction paper to fold over the top as a roof.

Put the houses on a table in two rows facing each other. The rows should be 6" (15 cm) apart. Label the road between the houses as Petersen Street.

Ask students to create an award to give each house (Brightest House, Very Red House, Smallest House).

Can You Flip Your Wig?

Review the story for the figurative language that is used to explain that Mr. Plumbean and his neighbors have gone too far.

Example: *flipped his wig*

            popped his cork

Illustrate a literal picture of each.

The Big Orange Splot

Provide each student with a piece of white construction paper. Put one teaspoon (5 ml) of orange paint in the center. Fold the paper. Gently rub the paper to move the paint to form a big orange splot.

Let the splot dry. Decorate and name your Big Orange Splot.

Related Readings

Read other books with figurative language: *The King Who Rained* by F. Gywnne, the Amelia Bedelia Books by P. Parish and *Owl Moon* by J. Yolen.

The Big Orange Splot

Color the splot orange. Make the splot into something interesting. Cut it out. Glue it onto orange paper. Let friends guess what it is and write it on the back.

Honesty Respect Responsibility Compassion Self-Discipline Perseverance Giving Friendship

Dribbles
Acceptance and Love

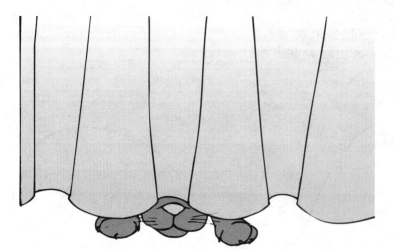

Summary

This beautiful but sad story is told from the cat's point of view. After Grandma dies, Grandpa and his old cat move in with the family and their three cats. It takes a long time for the cats to become friends. In the end, death brings sadness again.

Before Reading

Open the book cover so that students can see the complete picture on the front and back. Count the cats. Introduce Dribbles as the cat who is coming to join the family. Ask students why one cat is under the bed, and what they think the Siamese cat is saying to the black cat.

While Reading

📖 Read to the part of the story in which Dribbles jumps up on the old man's bed.

🛑 Ask the question again? Why is the cat under the bed? What do you think the Siamese cat is saying to the black cat? Who is the old man? Does he look okay? Why does he have a suitcase? What does Benny mean when he says, "I don't give up." Ask students if they ever feel like giving up?

📖 Read to the point of the story in which Dribbles returns looking very different.

🛑 Why does Dribbles return with her fur shaved off? Why she is named Dribbles?

📖 Read to the end of the story. Be prepared to read parts of this again to make sure students realize that Dribbles has died. Where is Dribbles being taken? What happened to the cat? How do the other cats feel? How does the old man feel? The cats are sad. How can Gracie say she feels better? Bing always says, "I know." How does this make the other cats feel? Do they feel the same way when he says it at the end of the story? Does anyone repeat things that irritate you? Discuss and ask why students feel or have felt that way.

After Reading

What values do students recognize in this story? What other stories are similar to this one? How are they different? What real-life incidents touch on the same issue?

Dribbles
Extension Activities

Happy, Sad, Scared, Lonely

Recall the events of the story with students. Record the events on the chalkboard. Discuss the characters' feelings at each point in the story. Label the events as *sad, happy, friendly, unfriendly, lonely* and *polite,* etc. If the students do not notice that all characters have different feelings, point this out.

Example: One cat was hiding under the bed. The cat under the bed felt: scared, panicked, frightened. Other cats looking at the cat felt: curious, wondering.

What's Next?

Ask students to draw a story telling what happened the next day with the family (old man, Benny, Bing and Gracie). Share the stories with the class.

Friendly and Unfriendly

Create a chart describing ways to show being friendly and unfriendly. First list events from the story. Then list other ways that students describe. Students can dramatize each of the friendly and unfriendly ways on the list in skits.

Honesty Respect Responsibility Compassion Self-Discipline Perseverance Giving Friendship

Jamaica Tag-Along
Hurt Feelings

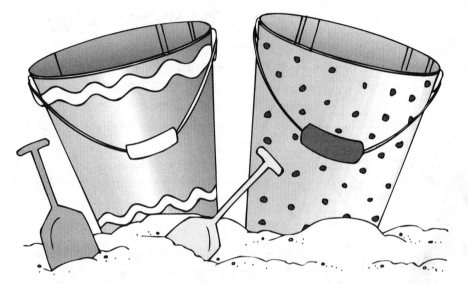

Summary

Jamaica wants to tag along with her big brother Ossie. But big kids don't like to be bothered by little kids. Then Jamaica plays with a younger boy in the sandpile and realizes she is treating him just like her brother treats her. She learns how to play together.

While Reading

Read to the part of the story in which Jamaica asks, "Can I come along, too?"

Should Ossie let Jamaica come along? Why? Why not?

Read to the point of the story in which Berto's mother's comments, "Big kids don't like to be bothered by little kids."

Why does Ossie tell Jamaica that he doesn't want her to tag along? Ask students how they would feel if they were Jamaica? If they were Ossie? Are Jamaica and Ossie right in feeling the way they do? Describe Jamaica's mood. Why is she feelings that way? Ask students how they would feel if they were Berto. What could make everyone's feelings change?

Turn to the page, but before reading, discuss the expression on Jamaica's face. Read to the end of the story. Suggest that students pay attention to the facial expressions and body language of each character.

Ask students if they would allow Ossie to help build the castle? Why? Why not? Describe their relationship now. What does it mean when Jamaica doesn't mind if Ossie tags along? What is the problem in this story? How is it solved? What could have been done to avoid the problem all together?

After Reading

What values do students recognize in this story? What other stories are similar to this one? How are they different? What real-life incidents touch on the same issue?

Honesty   Respect   Responsibility   Compassion   Self-Discipline   Perseverance   Giving   Friendship

Jamaica Tag-Along
Extension Activities

Feelings Web

Construct a feelings web on a piece of chart paper as shown below. Ask students to recall the story's events. Write them under the word *Events*. Ask students to identify the characters involved in the event. List how each character felt under the character label. Summarize each character.

Event	Characters		
	Jamaica	Ossie	Berto
Ossie tells Jamaica not to tag along.	upset	bossy	

How Do You Feel?

Dramatize the entire story. As students step in the shoes of a character, ask them to try to empathize with and understand the character. Take turns being different characters to show how they can be characterized differently.

Sandpile Fun

Using the sandpile on the playground or the sand table in the classroom, ask students to build sand walls and castles. Ask them to think abut how their feelings are not always the same when they knock the wall or castle down. If they want to change the building because they don't like it or want to build it differently, their feelings will not be the same as when someone comes by and wrecks it.

Honesty   Respect   Responsibility   Compassion   Self-Discipline   Perseverance   Giving   Friendship

Friendship

Giving

Perseverance

Self-Discipline

Compassion

Responsibility

Respect

Honesty

Little Monster at School
Finding New Friends

Summary

Little Monster tells about his day at school. Everyone is good at something except Yally, who doesn't like anything. He gets mad when others do things better than he does. When the children discover Yally is good at drawing pictures, they compliment him and make him feel special.

While Reading

📖 Read to the part of the story in which Yally is mad about Little Laff.

🛑 Ask students how they feel when someone does something better that they do. What will Yally do? What will Little Laff do?

📖 Read to the point of the story in which Yally's plant won't grow. He says it is mad at him.

🛑 Can a plant be mad at someone? Why does Yally think it is mad at him? What should Yally do to make his plant grow?

📖 Read to the point of the story in which Mr. Grithix reads a story.

🛑 How does Yally feel about the story? Why is he angry? How should Yally act if the teacher reads a story he doesn't want to hear?

📖 Read to the point of the story in which Yally draws a great picture.

🛑 What do the other children think of Yally's picture? How do they let him know? What could Little Laff have done?

📖 Finish the story.

🛑 Why is Yally so friendly now? What did the children do that made Yally feel good? Ask students what they can do to make their friends feel really good?

After Reading

What values do students recognize in this story? What other stories are similar to this one? How are they different? What real-life incidents touch on the same issues?

Little Monster at School
Extension Activities

Letter Trouble

Yally had trouble writing his letters. Ask students to make a chart for Yally to follow. Use a long strip of paper and place it vertically on the table. Ask students to write each letter as well as they can to show Yally the correct way to write. (For fun, let students use another strip to write the letters the way Yally did.)

Growing Power

Ask students to write a letter to Yally telling him how to take care of a plant. They should tell Yally what three things a plant needs to grow.

Younger children can draw the three pictures on folded paper. Write the title at the top, "Three Things to Help Plants Grow."

Pet Care

The children is this story took care of their pets. Ask students about pets they have at home, and how they care for them. Write or illustrate pages for a class book about pet care.

Pet Scramble

Unscramble these words to find the pets that belong to Little Monster and his friends.

uettrl _____

asertmh _____

tbarbi _____

hifs _____

easnk _____

iprmpuepz _____

Related Readings

Others have trouble in school, too. Read *Crow Boy*.

Friendship Giving Perseverance Self-Discipline Compassion Responsibility Respect Honesty

Mean Soup
Everyone Can Have a Bad Day

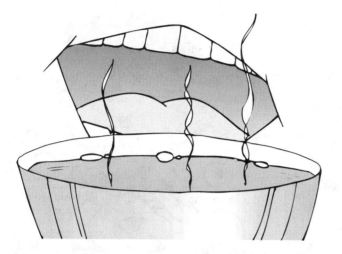

Summary

Horace has a bad day at school and comes home in a very bad mood. His mother helps him release his anger by making "mean" soup.

Before Reading

Predict who will make mean soup? Who will eat mean soup?

(Vertical text in left margin: Friendship Giving Perseverance Self-Discipline Compassion Responsibility Respect Honesty)

While Reading

📖 Read to the part of the story in which Horace arrives home in a mean mood after a bad day.

🛑 What bad things happen to Horace? Ask students what they would do if those things happened to them. Will stepping on the flower make Horace feel better? Why? Why not?

📖 Read to the point of the story in which Mother suggests they make soup, but Horace isn't interested.

🛑 How does Mother react to Horace's mood? Why does mother want to make soup? Look at the illustrations. What is mother doing? Why? How does Mother feel about Horace? How does he feel about Mother?

📖 Read to the point of the story in which Mother sticks out her tongue, and Horace sticks out his tongue 20 times.

🛑 Why do Mother and Horace scream into the pot? Why does he stick out his tongue 20 times? Will he feel better doing it 20 times instead of one time? Why? Why not?

📖 Finish the story.

🛑 How did making soup make Horace smile? What is the dog thinking? Ask students if they ever feel like they need to make mean soup? When?

After Reading

What values do students recognize in this story? What other stories are similar to this one? How are they different? What real-life incidents touch on the same issue?

Mean Soup
Extension Activities

Recipe for Mean Soup

Review the ingredients that Horace and his mother put in the soup. Make a list of measurement words such as *teaspoon, tablespoon, cup* and *quart*. Divide students into small groups. Give each group a piece of chart paper. As they write their recipe for Mean Soup, ask them to refer to the measurement words for ideas and spelling. Ask each group to share their recipe. Generate a list of cooking words that will help with ideas and spelling. The list may include *stir, mix, beat, slice, chop, dice, pour, bake, fry,* etc.

The Soup Pot

On a bulletin board, draw or cut out from construction paper a big black soup pot. Ask students to think of an ingredient from the story or supply other ideas of their own. Write the ideas on paper strips and curl the strips around a pencil. Attach them so they appear to be boiling out of the soup pot. Students may wish to call it Mean Soup or choose a name of their own.

What Happens Next?

Ask each student to draw and/or write a story telling what happens to Horace the next day.

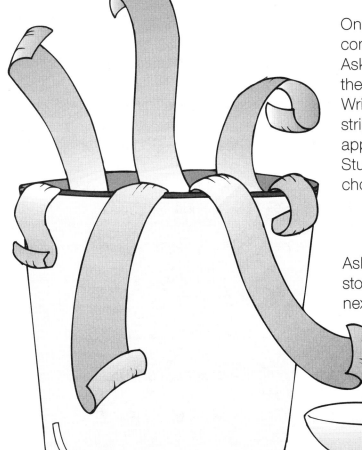

Bibliography

Clements, Andrew. (1988). *Big Al*. Ill. Yoshi. New York: Scholastic, Inc. ISBN: 0-590-44455-7

Everitt, Betsy. (1992). *Mean Soup*. Orlando, FL: Harcourt Brace & Co., Inc. ISBN: 0-440-83182-2

Gwynne, F. (1988). *The King Who Rained*. New York: Simon & Schuster. ISBN: 0-671-66363-1

Havill, Juanita. (1989). *Jamaica Tag-Along*. Ill. Anne Sibley O'Brien. New York: Houghton Mifflin Company. ISBN: 0-590-44062-4

Heckert, Connie. (1993). *Dribbles*. Ill. Elizabeth Sayles. New York: Clarion Books. ISBN: 0-395-62336-7

Lionni, Leo. (1963). *Swimmy*. New York: Alfred A. Knopf, Inc. ISBN: 0-590-43049-1

MacLachlan, Patricia. (1979). *Through Grandpa's Eyes*. New York: Harper & Row Publishers. ISBN: 0-06-024044X

Mayer, Mercer. (1994). *Little Monster at School*. (software). Green Frog Publishers, Inc. LOC#: 77-90845

Parish, P. (1992). *Amelia Bedelia*. New York: Harper & Row. ISBN: 0-06-444155-5

Parish, P. (1990). *Amelia Bedelia*. (audiocassette). Old Greenwich, CT: Listening Library.

Parish, P. (1981). *Amelia Bedelia and the Baby*. New York: Greenwillow Books. ISBN: 0-688-00321-4

Parish, P. (1966). *Amelia Bedelia and the Surprise Shower*. New York: Harper. ISBN: 0-06-024643-X

Parish, P. (1986). *Amelia Bedelia and the Surprise Shower*. (audiocassette). New York: Listening Library.

Parish, P. (1963). *Amelia Bedelia Goes Camping*. New York: Greenwillow Books. ISBN: 0-688-04057-8

Parish, P. (1963). *Amelia Bedelia Helps Out*. New York: Greenwillow Books. ISBN: 0-688-84231-3

Pfister, Marcus. (1992). *Rainbow Fish*. New York: Scholastic, Inc. ISBN: 0-590-48169-X

Pinkwater, Daniel Manus. (1977). *The Big Orange Splot*. New York: Scholastic, Inc. ISBN: 0-590-44510-3

Surat, Michele Maria. (1983). *Angel Child, Dragon Child*. New York: Scholastic, Inc. ISBN: 0-590-42271-5

Viorst, Judith. (1972). *Alexander and the Terrible, Horrible, No Good, Very Bad Day*. New York: Atheneum. ISBN: 0–689-70428-3

Viorst, Judith. (1984). *Alexander and the Terrible, Horrible, No Good, Very Bad Day*. (audiocassette). Caedmon Records.

Viorst, Judith. (1990). *Alexander and the Terrible, Horrible, No Good, Very Bad Day*. (videocassette). Western Publishing Company; Home Box Office.

Yashima, T. (1955). *Crow Boy*. New York: Viking Press. ISBN: 0-670-24931-9

Yolen, J. (1987). *Owl Moon*. New York: Philomel Books.

Yolen, J. (1990-1987). *Owl Moon*. Print Braille Edition. Boston: National Braille Press.

Yolen, J. (1987). *Owl Moon and Other Stories*. (videocassette). Los Angeles: Children's Circle Home Video.

Honesty Respect Responsibility Compassion Self-Discipline Perseverance Giving Friendship

TLC10071 Copyright © Teaching & Learning Company, Carthage, IL 62321-0010

Dear Parents,

This week we are studying about self-discipline, one of the virtues that Dr. Ernest Boyer suggests schools should examine. Dr. Boyer defines *self-discipline* as "Each person agrees to live within limits, not only the ones mutually agreed upon, but above all, those established personally. *Self-discipline* is exercised in relationships with others, especially in the way people speak to one another. Self-discipline also applies to the use of time. At the simplest level, self-control reflects habits of good living." Ernest Boyer, before his death late in 1995, served as U.S. Commissioner of Education and was president of The Carnegie Foundation for the Advancement of Teaching.

Several books for young children address *self-discipline*. These books include:

Apple Picking Time
Arthur's Teacher Trouble
Arthur's Thanksgiving
Arthur's Tooth
Arthur's Valentine
Babushka's Baba Yaga
Babushka's Doll
Baby Rattlesnake
The Dancing Granny
Galimoto
Keepers of the Animals
Keepers of the Earth
Keepers of Life
Keepers of the Night
The Keeping Quilt
Max and Ruby's Midas: Another Greek Myth
Thunder Cake
Tops & Bottoms
The Tortoise and the Hare

We will read some of these books in class.

Expect your child/children to use terms like *self-discipline, rules, limits* and *good use of time* in their conversations with you this week. You may have an opportunity to share your feelings with your child/children about *self-discipline*. Please feel free to call me with questions or concerns.

Sincerely,

Apple Picking Time
Responsibility and Fun for the Whole Family

Summary

Anna, Mama, Papa, Grandma and Grandpa work as pickers each year during the apple harvest. Anna shares the traditions her family celebrates during the harvest. A young child, she works to fill her bag, although it takes her all day. Perseverance and responsibility lead her to feelings of accomplishment as a half-moon is punched in her purple ticket which she can cash in at the barn.

Before Reading

This book can be tied to units on apples, families, harvest, gloves, grandparents, traditions, or quilts. Fall is a great time to talk with children about picking apples and about being responsible in completing tasks.

While Reading

Read to the part of the story in which the family goes to pick apples.

Before finding out what Anna's job will be while the family picks apples, ask these questions: What jobs do the family members have before harvest? What are their jobs during apple picking time? Do the adults and the children both have responsibilities? Are they the same responsibilities? What are their responsibilities?

Read to the point of the story in which they go back to picking apples after lunch.

Before Anna returns to picking, ask these questions: What does Anna want to accomplish? Will she accomplish it? Why? Why not?

Finish the story.

What is Anna's goal for this time? For the next time? Does Anna accomplish her goal this time? Does she next time? Why? Why not? Do all the people have the same goals? How do they feel when they finished the day? Ask students how they feel when they get things done?

After Reading

What values do students recognize in this story? What other stories are similar to this one? How are they different? What real-life incidents touch on the same issues?

Apple Picking Time
Extension Activities

Field Trip

Plan a field trip to an orchard. After explanations about how a harvest works, allow the children to pick fruit from the trees to eat.

Estimate How Many

Put bags of apples on an estimation table. Ask each student to guess how many apples are in each bag and write their guess on a recording sheet. Then ask them to count how many apples are in the bag and write their answer on their recording sheet. Students should try to figure out how far off they were with their estimates and which of their estimates was the closest.

Workers' Gloves

Examine the gloves of various occupations to investigate reasons why workers wear gloves.

Try picking up prickly things (pine needles, thistles, etc.) with and without different kinds of gloves. Determine which gloves offer the most protection.

Letter Pick Up

Provide students with lunch sacks and purple strips of paper. Each morning ask them to set a goal for the day. "How many sacks of litter will you pick up today?" At the end of the day, they must list the number of sacks they were able to fill. Punch their purple ticket once for each filled sack.

75

Arthur's Teacher Trouble
Preparation Wins the Day

help
need
care
play
smile

friend
give
learn
laugh
trust

Summary

The new third-grade teacher, Mr. Ratburn, is so mean that he gives homework on the very first day of school! Arthur and his friends wish they had a teacher who didn't make them study so hard. When Mr. Ratburn announces a spelling contest, Arthur meets the challenge and wins!

While Reading

📖 Read to the part of the story in which Arthur tells his mother that he has the strictest teacher in the whole world.

🛑 Should Arthur do his homework, even on the first day of school?

📖 Read to the point of the story in which Mr. Ratburn announces a spelling test on 100 words with the winner representing the class in the school's spellathon.

One hundred words! That's a lot of words to learn in a few days. Should Arthur try to get the best score so he can be in the spellathon? How should Arthur study for this test?

🛑 Read to the point of the story in which Mr. Ratburn gives Arthur and Brain 100 words to practice.

📖 How can Arthur's friends and family help him get ready for the contest? How will the friends feel? How will the family feel? How will Arthur feel?

🛑 Read to the part of the story in which it is the day of the spellathon. Brain feels fine but Arthur wishes he is back in bed.

📖 Arthur is nervous about the test. Why? What should he do?

🛑 Finish the book.

📖 How does D.W. feel about having Mr. Ratburn for a teacher? What does she do to show how she feels? What advice should Arthur give her?

After Reading

What values do students recognize in this story? What other stories are similar to this one? How are they different? What real-life incidents touch on the same issues?

Arthur's Teacher Trouble
Extension Activities

Spellathon

Hold a spellathon using these words about friendship. Discuss what the words have to do with being a good friend.

friend	help	understand
smile	trust	need
give	cry	patience
fun	care	
play	learn	

Study Habits

Arthur's friends have different ways of studying their spelling words. How many different ways of studying are in the book? List more ways to study spelling words. Which one seems to be the best way?

Writing Activity

Write a letter to Arthur congratulating him for winning the spellathon.

Personal Teacher Trouble

Have the children tell you different ways they are in trouble with their current teacher. How many compare to Arthur's troubles? Do the children say why there is trouble when these things happen?

Related Readings

Read more about Arthur in Marc Brown's books such as *Arthur's Valentine, Arthur's Tooth* and *Arthur's Thanksgiving*.

Babushka's Doll
Impatience and Selfishness Doesn't Always Work

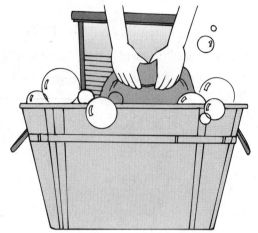

Summary

Natasha is a very impatient, selfish child. She expects her grandmother (Babushka) to respond to her requests immediately. Natasha becomes acquainted with Babushka's doll but only plays with it once. When she tries to play with the doll, the doll treats her naughtily. This upsets Natasha, and she learns a lesson from it.

Before Reading

Discuss the meaning of the word *Babushka*.

While Reading

📖 Read to the part of the story in which Babushka is washing the laundry and asks Natasha for help.

🛑 Look at Natasha's face. How is she talking to her grandmother? What is she saying?

📖 Read to the point of the story in which Babushka is feeding the goats and tells Natasha not to be selfish.

🛑 Why does Babushka call Natasha? What could Natasha have done instead? Has anyone in this classroom ever been selfish? How did others feel?

📖 Read to the part of the story in which Natasha notices the doll on the shelf when she and Babushka are having lunch.

🛑 Why did Natasha only play with the doll once?

📖 Read to the part of the story in which the doll begins to dance and wants Natasha to play.

🛑 Look at Natasha's face. How does she feel? Will they play together and have a good time? Why? Why not?

📖 Read to the part of the story in which Natasha wishes the doll was just a doll.

🛑 Why does Natasha tell Babushka that the doll was naughty? Did it really happen or was it just a bad dream? Why? Why not?

📖 Finish the book.

🛑 Why do you think Natasha only played with the doll once? Did Babushka's doll really come to life or did Natasha imagine it?

After Reading

What values do students recognize in this story? What other stories are similar to this one? How are they different? What real-life incidents touch on the same issue?

Babushka's Doll
Extension Activities

Puppets for Play

Place tracing paper over the pictures in the story of Natasha, Babushka and the doll. Trace the characters. Color them in. Use these puppets while telling the story. Place them in a center for the students to use while retelling the story and experience selfishness.

Create a Story

Ask students to write and illustrate a story about selfishness. Provide a selection of material (folded paper, blank books, story writing paper, etc.). Ask them to start with pictures or writing. Some may choose to make puppets. Share their stories at sharing time.

Doll in the Dollhouse

Usually the best thing to do with dolls in the dollhouse or housekeeping area is to provide several so there is no conflict. For the purpose of exploring selfishness, remove all but the one doll from the center. While observing, interject questions: "Only one doll today?" "How's it working with only one doll today?" "What in the world will happen with only one doll to play with today?"

Related Readings

Read *Thunder Cake* and *The Keeping Quilt*, Polacco stories about Babushka.

Baby Rattlesnake
Learning a Lesson

Summary

Baby Rattlesnake cried because he was too young to have rattles. When the elders finally gave him rattles, he used them to scare the other animals. When Baby Rattlesnake used the rattles to scare the chief's daughter, she smashed his rattles and taught him a lesson.

Before Reading

Teachers should read the section at the end of the book about this Chickasaw folktale for their own information. Discuss the importance of storytelling in any culture with students before sharing this story.

While Reading

📖 Read to the part of the story in which Mother and Father Rattlesnake will not allow Baby Rattlesnake to have rattles.

🛑 Discuss rules that parents make to keep children safe. Examples: Do not cross the street without an adult. Do not play with fire. Why do parents make these rules?

📖 Read to the point of the story in which Baby Rattlesnake uses his rattles to scare the other animals.

🛑 Why do Mother and Father Rattlesnake tell Baby this is not a good way to use his rattles?

📖 Finish the story.

🛑 How does Baby Rattlesnake feel when he loses the rattles? Does Baby Rattlesnake learn his lesson? What could have happened to Baby Rattlesnake instead of losing his rattles?

After Reading

What values do students recognize in this story? What other stories are similar to this one? How are they different? What real-life incidents touch on the same issue?

80

Baby Rattlesnake
Extension Activities

Safety First

Ask students to help make a list of safety rules to follow. Discuss why each rule is important to remember.

Learning About Rattlesnakes

Share pictures of rattlesnakes with students. Discuss how a real rattlesnake uses its rattles to protect itself. Have students draw pictures of Baby Rattlesnake with a new set of rattles.

Rules for Baby Snakes

1. Baby Rattlesnakes should
2. Baby Rattlesnakes

Rules for Baby Snakes

Ask students to help write safety rules for Baby Rattlesnake. Place them on poster board. Make a border of Native American patterns, lines, circles, zigzags.

Examples:

Baby Rattlesnakes should not cross the highway.

Baby Rattlesnakes should not eat light bulbs or other objects they don't recognize.

Related Readings

Read other Native American folktales. A good collection can be found in Michael Caduto's books, *Keepers of the Animals* and *Keepers of the Earth*.

Galimoto
The Result of Perseverance and Self-Discipline

Summary

Kondi has saved things for a long time for something special. It was time for him to make his galimoto, but he did not have enough wire. He did, however, want to make his own galimoto. He took the things he had, traded for other things, asked for scrap wire, found some wire in a trash pile and was ready to shape his galimoto. Even then it took self-discipline and perseverance to complete the task.

Before Reading

From the cover illustration, have students guess what the young boy is doing.

While Reading

📖 Read to the part of the story in which the boy tells Kondi that he doesn't have enough wire.

🛑 How does the older boy know that Kondi doesn't have enough wire? Kondi has been saving for a long time for something special. If Kondi doesn't have enough wire, what could he do?

📖 Read to the point of the story in which Kondi runs into more difficulties. Stop after each one.

🛑 Ask students what Kondi's options are each time a problem arises.

📖 Finish the story.

🛑 Who told Kondi to make the galimoto? Who told him how? Who was in charge? How did he feel? When Kondi decides he is ready to make his galimoto, he finds he does have enough wire. How does he feel? Why doesn't that stop him from making the galimoto? Ask students if they have wanted to do something that took them some time to finish even when others said it couldn't be done. How did that feel?

After Reading

What values do students recognize in this story? What other stories are similar to this one? How are they different? What real-life incidents touch on the same issues?

Honesty   Respect   Responsibility   Compassion   Self-Discipline   Perseverance   Giving   Friendship

82

Galimoto
Extension Activities

Wheels

Provide students with clear plastic, zip-type bags. Ask them to collect things for a week or two that will make good wheels. One afternoon, ask them to shape wheels out of the materials. Roll the wheels down a ramp to see which ones work the best.

If the students are interested, ask them to decide what else they need and continue saving for another workday.

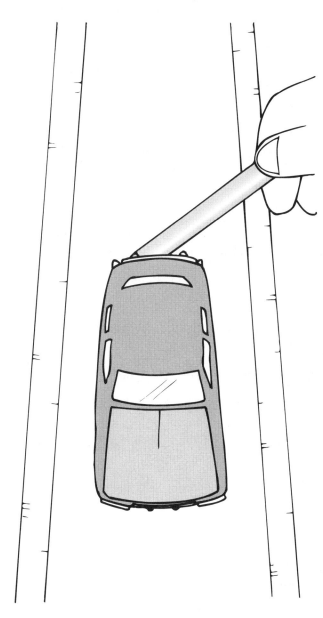

Push Car Obstacle Course

Place a masking tape track on the floor in an open area of the room. Ask students to choose a toy car and a stick (piece of dowel rod) from a box of cars and assorted sticks. Their challenge is to push the cars around the track with the sticks, staying on the path as closely as possible.

For those who are successful, the next challenge is pushing two cars with two sticks at the same time. Challenge them with other feats.

Tie a string to a car, pull the car and try to follow the track. Which is easier? Why?

Tube Push

Decorate toilet paper, paper towel and wrapping paper tubes. Provide pushing sticks to help students push their tubes from one place to another.

Max and Ruby's Midas:
Another Greek Myth
Too Much of a Good Thing

Summary

Max would rather eat sweets than nourishing food, so Ruby reads a story to him about a boy named Midas. Midas turned all the good food into sweets and candy. When he turned his family into foods he was all alone. Midas learned the lesson that you can have too much of a good thing, but Max still hasn't learned to stop eating cupcakes.

Before Reading

What kinds of foods are good for growing children? What kinds of food are not good? Ask students if they have ever eaten too much candy? How did they feel afterward?

While Reading

📖 Read to the part of the story in which Ruby says she sees and hears Max.

🛑 Why does Max call the cupcake beautiful? Why does Max hide the cupcakes?

📖 Read to the point of the story in which Max discovers he has changed his family into ice cream and gelatin.

🛑 What has happened to Max's family? Why is he unhappy? What should he do to get his family back?

📖 Read to the point of the story in which Ruby says good night to Max.

🛑 Discuss what it means to have too much of a good thing. Ask if Max has learned a lesson from Midas's story?

📖 Finish the story.

🛑 Does Max learn his lesson?

After Reading

What values do students recognize in this story? What other stories are similar to this one? How are they different? What real-life incidents touch on the same issue?

Self-Discipline

Honesty Respect Responsibility Compassion Perseverance Giving Friendship

Max and Ruby's Midas: Another Greek Myth
Extension Activities

Mythology

Explain what a myth is. Share other stories from Greek mythology. Use *One Minute Myths* by Sheri Lewis to get students started.

Food from Around the World

Locate the United States and Greece on a world map or globe.

Draw or find pictures of the foods described in this book.

Cut out and attach the pictures of American foods on a map or drawing of the United States. Cut out and paste the pictures of the Greek foods on a map or drawing of Greece.

Take a Sweet Tooth Poll

List 10 favorite sweets. Ask each student to survey his or her family to see which sweets are their favorites. Place a sticker for each vote beside the sweet to make a bar graph and show which sweets are liked the most. (See the following page for a recording sheet.)

Honesty   Respect   Responsibility   Compassion   Self-Discipline   Perseverance   Giving   Friendship

Too Many Sweets
Interview and Recording Sheet

1. Write the name of your favorite candies in the top box on the left.
2. Write your name in the upper right-hand corner in the box.
3. Interview your family members.
4. Ask them to write their favorite candy and their name in the other boxes.
   Share the results with your friends at school.

Friendship · Giving · Perseverance · Self-Discipline · Compassion · Responsibility · Respect · Honesty

Tops & Bottoms
A Trickster Tale

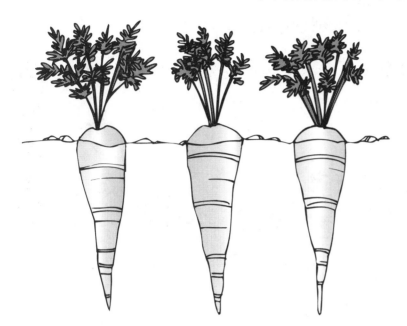

Summary

Bear has mor[e] is too lazy to [work?]. The Hare fa[mily] and no land. The Hares convince Bear to let them grow vegetables on his land and split the crop in half. Bear is too busy sleeping to figure out how the Hares trick him out of his crop each year. When Bear finally decides to wake up and work his own land, both Bear and the Hare family earn a profit.

Before Reading

Before taking a field trip to the farm, ask students to make a list of questions about how farms work. Take a field trip to a farm or show pictures of farmers growing food. Discuss how hard farmers have to work to make things grow.

While Reading

📖 Read to the part of the story in which Father Hare decides something must be done to feed his hungry children.

🛑 Ask students what the Hare family could do to get some food. How can Mother and Father Hare earn their food?

📖 Read to the point of the story in which Hares gather both the tops and the bottoms of the crop and agree to give them to Bear.

🛑 What will the Hares do now that Bear gets the whole crop? Will the Hares grow a crop just for Bear? What are various ways that the Hares and Bear can work this problem out?

📖 Finish the story.

🛑 What lesson does Bear learn from the Hares? Will Bear go back to being lazy? Who would be the best to live with, Bear or the Hares? Why?

After Reading

What values do students recognize in this story? What other stories are similar to this one? How are they different? What real-life incidents touch on the same issues?

Tops & Bottoms
Extension Activities

Art Activity

Make two lists of vegetables. In one column write the names of vegetables that produce food in the tops. In the other list, write the names of vegetables that produce food in the bottoms. Use the pictures and story to help make the list. Ask each student to choose a favorite vegetable to illustrate.

Digging for Potatoes

Place potatoes, beets, carrots and onions in the sand table. Cover with sand. Ask students to dig for them.

The Hare's Veggie Stand

Set up a make-believe vegetable stand in the dramatic play area with the sign, *Mrs. Hare's Fruits and Vegetables.* Use plastic fruits and vegetables, play money, an apron for Mrs. Hare and overalls for Mr. Hare. Discuss what it takes to be successful in a business and courteous to customers.

Planting Seeds

Plant bean or radish seeds in clear plastic cups with students. Fill the paper cups with soil and water the seeds often. When the seedlings break through the soil and sprout leaves, carefully take the seedlings out of the dirt and inspect the roots. Plant the seedlings in a garden or in the cups for students to take home and transplant.

88

Bibliography

Ata, Te. (1989). *Baby Rattlesnake*. San Francisco, CA: Children's Book Press. ISBN: 0-89239-049-2

Brown, Marc. (1989). *Arthur's Teacher Trouble*. New York: Little, Brown & Company. ISBN: 0-316-11186-4

Brown, Marc. (1986). *Arthur's Teacher Trouble*. (audiocassette). Canada: Little, Brown & Company.

Brown, Marc. (1986). *Arthur's Teacher Trouble*. (CD-ROM). Canada: Little, Brown & Company.

Brown, M.T. (1983). *Arthur's Thanksgiving*. New York: Little, Brown & Company. ISBN: 0-316-11060-4

Brown, M.T. (1985). *Arthur's Tooth*. New York: Little, Brown & Company. ISBN: 0-316-11246-1

Brown, M.T. (1980). *Arthur's Valentine*. New York: Little, Brown & Company. ISBN: 0-316-11187-2

Bryan, Ashley. (1977). *The Dancing Granny*. New York: Simon & Schuster. ISBN: 0-689-71149-2

Caduto, M.J. (1994). *Keepers of Life*. Golden, CO: Fulcrum Publishers. ISBN: 1-55591-186-2

Caduto, M.J. (1991). *Keepers of the Animals*. Golden, CO: Fulcrum Publishers. ISBN: 1-55591-088-2

Caduto, M.J. (1988). *Keepers of the Earth*. Golden, CO: Fulcrum Publishers. ISBN: 1-55591-027-0

Caduto, M.J. (1994). *Keepers of the Night*. Golden, CO: Fulcrum Publishers.

Polacco, Patricia. (1993). *Babushka Baba Yaga*. New York: Philomel. ISBN: 0-399-22531-5

Polacco, Patricia. (1990). *Babushka's Doll*. New York: Simon & Schuster Books for Young Readers. ISBN: 0-590-62205-6

Polacco, Patricia. (1988). *The Keeping Quilt*. New York: Simon & Schuster Books for Young Readers. ISBN: 0-671-64963-9

Polacco, Patricia. (1990). *Thunder Cake*. New York: Philomel Books. ISBN: 0-399-22231-6

Schlichting, Mark. (1993). *The Tortoise and the Hare*. (with CD-ROM). Broderbund.

Slawson, Michele Benoit. (1994). *Apple Picking Time*. New York: Crown Publishers, Inc. ISBN: 0-517-58971-0

Adapted and illustrated by Stevens, Janet. (1995). *Tops & Bottoms*. New York: Harcourt Brace & Company. ISBN: 0-15-292851-0

The Tortoise & the Hare. Children's Video Library. (1987). (videocassette). Hill of Fire/Great Plains National Instructional Television Library and WNED-TV. Produced by Lancit Media Productions. Children's Video Library. (Closed captioned)

Stevens, Janet. (1984). *The Tortoise and the Hare: An Aesop Fable*. New York: Holiday House. ISBN: 0-8234-0564-8

Stevens, Janet. (1985). *The Tortoise and the Hare*. (audiocassette). Listening Library.

Wells, Rosemary. (1995). *Max and Ruby's Midas: Another Greek Myth*. New York: Penguin Books. ISBN: 0-8037-1782-2

Williams, Karen Lynn. (1990). *Galimoto*. New York: Lothrop, Lee & Shepard Books. ISBN: 0-688-10991-8

Dear Parents,

This week we are studying about *perseverance*, one of the virtues that Dr. Ernest Boyer suggests schools should examine. Dr. Boyer defines *perseverance* as "Each person is diligent, with the inner strength and determination to pursue well-defined goals. It does matter that a task be completed once begun, and to persevere not only teaches discipline, but brings rewards as well. Each person pushes hard to complete assignments, and all members of the community willingly support others in their work." Ernest Boyer, before his death late in 1995, served as U.S. Commissioner of Education and was president of The Carnegie Foundation for the Advancement of Teaching.

Several books for young children address *perseverance*. These books include:

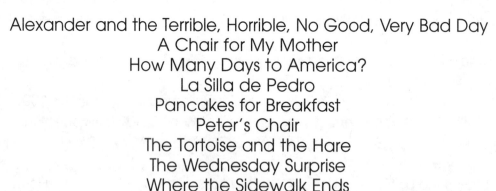

Alexander and the Terrible, Horrible, No Good, Very Bad Day
A Chair for My Mother
How Many Days to America?
La Silla de Pedro
Pancakes for Breakfast
Peter's Chair
The Tortoise and the Hare
The Wednesday Surprise
Where the Sidewalk Ends

We will read some of these books in class.

Expect your child to use terms like *stick to it, finish what you have started, diligent, determined* and *goals* in their conversations with you this week. You may have an opportunity to share your feelings with your child/children about *perseverance*. Please feel free to call with questions and concerns.

Sincerely,

Alexander and the Terrible, Horrible, No Good, Very Bad Day
When Things Go Wrong

Summary

Everything seems to go wrong for Alexander. He gets into fights with his brothers, has trouble in school, spills ink on his father's desk and even has to wear his railroad-train pajamas. Alexander wishes he was someplace else like Australia, but his mother says that some days are just like that, even in Australia.

Before Reading

Discuss how everyone has days in which things go wrong. Talk about how it makes a teacher feel after a day like that. What can children do to turn things around? How can they help someone who is having a bad day?

While Reading

📖 Read to the part of the story in which Alexander's day begins.

🛑 Discuss how Alexander feels at the breakfast table. What are the clues that show how he feels? How do his brothers feel?

📖 Read to the point of the story in which Paul says someone else is his best friend.

🛑 Discuss Alexander's response to Paul. Why does he say he hopes Paul sits on a tack? Do people ever say things they really don't mean?

📖 Finish the story.

🛑 Discuss how the next day could go for Alexander. What could Alexander do to make the next day go better? What does he do that could make the next day just as bad? Ask students to identify one thing Alexander decides to do, and tell what he could have done instead. How could things have gone differently?

After Reading

What values do students recognize in this story? What other stories are similar to this one? How are they different? What real-life incidents touch on the same issues?

Friendship · Giving · Perseverance · Self-Discipline · Compassion · Responsibility · Respect · Honesty

Alexander and the Terrible, Horrible, No Good, Very Bad Day
Extension Activities

A Good Citizen

Alexander has a bad day at school. List the things that go wrong and then list what Alexander could do to make his day at school go well. Use this list to make a poster for the classroom on how to be a good citizen at school.

Picture That!

Show pictures of vegetables. Talk about the nutrients in each food. Ask students to draw a picture of one of the vegetables. Caption the picture with something positive about that food. For example, draw a picture of broccoli with the caption, *Broccoli has many vitamins that make me healthy!*

Role Playing

Divide the class into small groups. Assign a scene from the book to each small group. Ask each group to role-play that scene. Or ask the group to think up a different ending for that scene and present it to the whole class.

Broccoli has many vitamins that make me healthy.

A Chair for My Mother
Working for What We Want

Summary

After they lose all their furniture in a fire, a child, her waitress mother and her grandmother save their money to buy a big comfortable chair.

Before Reading

Discuss what chairs are used for and how important a chair can be to a family. Ask students what they would do if there were no chairs in the house?

While Reading

📖 Read to the part of the story in which the child and her family need a chair.

🛑 Why do people leave a tip for a waiter or waitress? What do waiters and waitresses do with their tips?

📖 Read to the point of the story in which the events of the fire are explained.

🛑 Discuss fire safety and the importance of having an escape route and a meeting place outside. Ask students to discuss how others can help out when catastrophes happen.

📖 Finish the story.

🛑 Check to see if any of the students' responses match those of the author. Discuss how people can help when someone they know loses their home and possessions in a fire. Share a newspaper article or story about a house fire.

After Reading

What values do students recognize in this story? What other stories are similar to this one? How are they different? What real-life incidents touch on the same issues?

Perseverance Giving Friendship Self-Discipline Compassion Responsibility Respect Honesty

A Chair for My Mother
Extension Activities

Friendship · Giving · Perseverance · Self-Discipline · Compassion · Responsibility · Respect · Honesty

Design a Chair

Ask each student to draw a picture of a chair for the child and her family. The chair should be large and comfortable. Ask students to caption the chair, showing its use. For example, *My chair is for reading and taking a nap.*

Counting Coins

Fill a jar with pennies or coins. Hold a contest to guess how many coins are in the jar, then take turns counting the coins. Each child should record the number of coins they have counted. How many get the same number?

Ask students to bring in a penny each day. How long will it take to fill up the jar? Count the money. What can they purchase with the money?

Good Neighbors

List ways people can be good neighbors to each other. Start by listing what the neighbors did for the family in this story. Collect news articles about helping others and make a collage to go with the list.

Related Readings

Read Ezra Jack Keats' book, *Peter's Chair*.

How Many Days to America?
Day after day the question is, "How many days to America?"

Summary

A group of people are forced to leave their homeland. Many people have had to do this in the past. The young people keep asking the traditional question, "Are we there yet?" "How many days to America? "Not many" and "More" are the only answers they get until they finally arrive on Thanksgiving Day. They realize they have much to be thankful for.

While Reading

Read to the part of the story in which the family decides they must leave behind all they own in order to go to America.

STOP Who goes on the trip? What do they have to leave behind? Ask students what they would leave behind. How does the group of people feel? How do the students think they would feel? Would they decide to go or stay? Why?

Finish the story.

STOP How does the family feel when they see people waiting on the dock to welcome them to America? How do these new people feel about the boat people when they arrive and tell of their trip to America? How do the little children feel when they arrive to see these strange people? What could make the children feel safe?

After Reading

What values do students recognize in this story? What other stories are similar to this one? How are they different? What real-life incidents touch on the same issues?

Friendship Giving Perseverance Self-Discipline Compassion Responsibility Respect Honesty

How Many Days to America?
Extension Activities

How Many Days?

Place an upcoming event on the calendar. Each day have students ask, "How many days until _____?" Count the days.

Older students may enjoy being told they are going to have a pizza party soon. Each day have them ask, "How many days until the pizza party?" For several days say, "More" or "Not many," until the pizzas arrive. Discuss how knowing when something is going to happen and how not knowing when something is going to happen affects waiting.

What's for Dinner?

Send home a copy of the interview sheet on page 97. Ask students to interview their families about what they traditionally have for Thanksgiving dinner.

Record the results on a class graph, noting similarities and differences.

How Many Miles?

Locate America on a map. Locate other places in the world. Determine by the legend/mileage scale how many miles it is from one place to another.

Use local maps and ask students to determine how far one place is from another. At six miles a day by covered wagon, or 60 miles an hour, how far is it by highway or by an overland direct route (as the crow flies)?

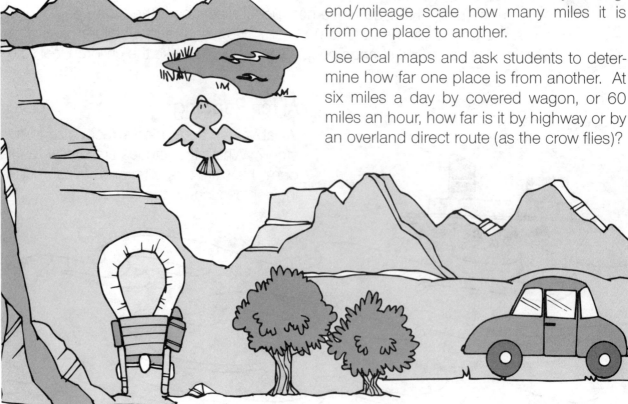

96

Name _____

Thanksgiving Dinner
Family Interview Sheet

Draw pictures of the foods that your family traditionally has for Thanksgiving dinner. Label each picture.

Friendship

Giving

Perseverance

Self-Discipline

Compassion

Responsibility

Respect

Honesty

Please return this sheet to school on _____.

Pancakes for Breakfast
If at First You Don't Succeed, Try, Try Again

Summary

A woman decides to make pancakes. She gathers eggs, churns butter and buys syrup until she has assembled all the ingredients. But the cat and dog eat the ingredients. So she visits a neighbor who is cooking pancakes and finally satisfies her appetite.

Before Reading

Discuss the importance of following directions when cooking. Share some examples of how a prepared food can turn out if the cook doesn't follow the recipe. Talk about why it is important to have all the ingredients gathered before you start to cook.

While Reading

Read to the part of the story in which the pancake recipe is found.

STOP What ingredients does she need to make pancakes?

Read to the point of the story in which she churns the butter.

STOP Discuss how farmers used to churn cream to make butter. Use the clock in the pictures to figure out how long it takes for her to make the butter.

Finish the story.

STOP Use the clock at the end of the book to figure out how long it takes the woman to get her pancakes. Discuss the saying on the wall displayed at the end of the book. What does it mean to keep trying until you succeed?

After Reading

What values do students recognize in this story? What other stories are similar to this one? How are they different? What real-life incidents touch on the same issues?

98

Honesty Respect Responsibility Compassion Self-Discipline Perseverance Giving Friendship

Pancakes for Breakfast
Extension Activities

Following Directions

Invite a cook to the class to discuss why it is important to follow directions carefully. Discuss what a cook does when a mistake is made. Does everything the cook makes turn out just right? How does the cook learn from mistakes?

Hard Workers

Make a list of foods students eat that come from a farm. Take a trip to a farm that raises food. Learn how much work is involved in producing food for peoples' breakfast meals. When the class returns to school, ask students to draw a sequence picture illustrating how a favorite food is produced. For example, the sequence picture for scrambled eggs could show a farmer feeding chickens, chickens laying eggs, the farmer collecting eggs, cleaning eggs, packaging eggs, trucking eggs to market, a customer buying eggs and preparing eggs.

Cooking Class

Ask students to find pancake recipes in cookbooks. Compare the ingredients in each recipe. Make pancakes. Assign tasks to small groups. Use the ideas for badges below.

Possible task assignments:

_____	Make the shopping list	_____	Set the table
_____	Assemble the ingredients	_____	Serve the pancakes
_____	Measure the ingredients	_____	Eat the pancakes
_____	Mix the ingredients	_____	Clear the table
_____	Cook the pancakes	_____	Clean up

Related Readings

For books about pancakes, read *Too Many Pancakes* and Shel Silverstein's poem, "Pancake" in *Where the Sidewalk Ends*.

The Tortoise and the Hare
Winning the Race

Summary

The hare is very busy and fast. The tortoise is very slow and deliberate. When the tortoise challenges the hare to a race, being slow and careful helps the tortoise win.

Before Reading

Discuss other names for a hare and a tortoise. Hares and rabbits are closely related. However, Hares give birth to young with fur and have black on the points of their ears. Rabbits' babies are furless and have no black on their ears. Rabbits burrow; hares do not. Turtles and tortoises are also closely related.

While Reading

📖 Read to the part of the story in which Hare makes fun of Tortoise because he listens to the birds sing and lies around.

🛑 How does Tortoise feel? How should a person act if someone makes fun of her or him? What could the Hare have said instead?

📖 Read to the point of the story in which Hare stops to show off some of his favorite moves.

🛑 What does it look like when someone is showing off? Why did Hare show off instead of running? How do people feel about someone who shows off? What could Hare have done differently? Did Tortoise decide to be just like Hare? Why not?

📖 Read to the part of the story in which Tortoise runs into many obstacles and falls behind in the race.

🛑 Is Tortoise working hard to get over the obstacles? What are some of the things that Tortoise can do when he gets far behind in the race?

📖 Finish the story.

🛑 How should Hare act when he loses the race? How should the Tortoise act when he wins?

After Reading

What values do students recognize in this story? What other stories are similar to this one? How are they different? What real-life incidents touch on the same issues?

TLC10071 Copyright © Teaching & Learning Company, Carthage, IL 62321-0010

The Tortoise and the Hare
Extension Activities

Obstacle Course

Create an obstacle course on the playground. Have students go through the obstacle course and time their performance. Then encourage each child to compete against his or her own time, not the times of the other students.

Racing Facts

List as many different kinds of races as the class can think of. Help students make a list of steps necessary to get ready for a race. Invite a speaker to visit the class and talk about training for one kind of race, or visit a local school sports program so students may watch and learn.

Related Readings

Read more of Aesop's fables.

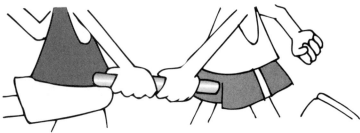

Hare and Tortoise Moving Along

Hare has many favorite moves. He can skip, jump, hop, sprint, spring and lope. Ask students to illustrate Hare and Tortoise's moves. Then ask students to take turns acting out the pictures they illustrated. Pictures should be labeled with the word that is illustrated.

Honesty   Respect   Responsibility   Compassion   Self-Discipline   Perseverance   Giving   Friendship

The Wednesday Surprise
With Much Hard Work, Grandma Will Read

Summary

Grandma and Anna work on a special surprise for Dad's birthday each Wednesday. Anna's mother stays late at the office, Sam goes to basketball practice and Dad is out of town. When the others get home, practice stops and the family enjoys other things together. When Dad's birthday comes, Grandma reads a story to the family–another and another. Dad, eyes brimming with tears, asks if she plans to read everything in her bag.

Before Reading

Ask students to describe the illustration on the front of the book (Grandma, Anna and the cat look at a book on a sofa, covered with a blanket), and relate it to their own lives.

While Reading

📖 Read only the first paragraph, when Anna and Grandma plan the best surprise of all for Dad's birthday.

🛑 Ask students what they think the surprise is. What gift would they give Dad on his birthday?

📖 Read to the point of the story in which Grandma arrives with a lumpy bag.

🛑 What is in the bag? Ask students what their grandmother brings with her to their homes.

📖 Finish the book.

🛑 What does Anna and her grandmother give to Dad? Is it a good surprise? Why?

After Reading

What values do students recognize in this story? What other stories are similar to this one? How are they different? What real-life incidents touch on the same issues?

Friendship Giving Perseverance Self-Discipline Compassion Responsibility Respect Honesty

102

The Wednesday Surprise
Extension Activities

What's in the Bag?

Every day pack a bag with different things. When the class meets for a demonstration or direct instruction lesson, ask students to guess what is in the bag.

Provide bags for students to use in the dramatic play or science area. There they can hide things in a bag and ask others to guess what is in the bag.

Character Books

Ask students to write the name of each character at the top of a page. Then ask students to draw pictures of each character on the appropriate page.

Ask older students to write a description of the characters at the bottom of each page. Younger children can write word descriptors for of each character. The youngest can cut pictures out, put a piece of felt on the back and use the characters on a felt board.

Birthday Dinner

Give each student a paper place mat. Ask students to design their own birthday dinner and to draw the place mat appropriately set with silverware, dishes and a glass.

Compare the students' meals with Anna's.

Give each student a piece of paper folded into nine boxes. Ask students to copy the foods in their meal onto the folded paper, one item per box. Ask students to write their name on the back of each box. Cut out the boxes. Graph the students' favorite birthday meals.

Bibliography

Bunting, Eve. (1988). *How Many Days to America?* New York: Clarion Books. ISBN: 0-395-54777-6

Bunting, Eve. (1989). *The Wednesday Surprise.* New York: Clarion Books. ISBN: 0-89919-721-3

De Paola, Tomie. (1978). *Pancakes for Breakfast.* New York: Harcourt Brace & Jovanovich, Inc. ISBN: 0-590-45136-7

Keats, E.J. (1967). *Peter's Chair.* New York: Harper & Row. ISBN: 0-06-023112-2

Keats, E.J. (1995). *Peter's Chair.* (audiocassette). New York: HarperCollins. ISBN: 0-694-70009-6

Keats, E.J. (1993). *Peter's Chair.* (Big Book Edition). New York: HarperCollins. ISBN: 0-06-443325-0

Keats, E.J. (1996). *La Silla de Pedro.* New York: Harper Arco Iris.

Keats, E.J. (1987). *Keats' Stories About Peter.* (videocassette). Weston, CT: Weston Woods Studios.

The Tortoise and the Hare. Retold by Mark Schlichting (1993). (software). Broderbund.

Stevens, Janet. (1984). *The Tortoise and the Hare: An Aesop Fable.* New York: Holiday House. ISBN: 0-8234-0564-8

Stevens, Janet. (1985). *The Tortoise and the Hare.* (audiocassette). Listening Library.

Children's Video Library. (1987). *The Tortoise and the Hare.* (videocassette). Hill of Fire/Great Plains National Instructional Television Library and WNED-TV. Produced by Lancit Media Productions. Children's Video Library. (Closed captioned).

Silverstein, Shel. (1992). *Where the Sidewalk Ends.* (CD). New York: Sony Music Entertainment.

Silverstein, Shel. (1984). *Where the Sidewalk Ends.* (audiocassette). New York: Columbia.

Viorst, Judith. (1972). *Alexander and the Terrible, Horrible, No Good, Very Bad Day.* Hartford, CT: Atheneum. ISBN: 0-689-70428-3

Viorst, Judith. (1984). *Alexander and the Terrible, Horrible, No Good, Very Bad Day.* (audiocassette). Caedmon Records.

Viorst, Judith. (screenplay and lyrics). (1990). *Alexander and the Terrible, Horrible, No Good, Very Bad Day.* (videocassette). Western Publishing Company; Home Box Office.

Williams, V.B. (1982). *A Chair for My Mother.* New York: Greenwillow Books. ISBN: 0-688-04074-8

Williams, V.B. (1986). *A Chair for My Mother.* (audiocassette). Listening Library.

TLC10071 Copyright © Teaching & Learning Company, Carthage, IL 62321-0010

Dear Parents,

This week we are studying about *giving,* one of the virtues that Dr. Ernest Boyer suggests schools should examine. Dr. Boyer defines *giving* as "Each person discovers that one of life's greatest satisfactions comes from giving to others, and recognizes that talents should be shared, through service. Rather than waiting to be asked, members of the community look for opportunities to respond positively to the needs of others, without expectation of reward." Ernest Boyer, before his death late in 1995, served as U.S. Commissioner of Education and was president of The Carnegie Foundation for the Advancement of Teaching.

Several books for young children address *giving.* These books include:

Alejandro's Gift
Angel Child, Dragon Child
The Doorbell Rang
How Many Days to America?
The Little Mouse, the Red Ripe Strawberry and
the Big Hungry Bear
The Legend of the Bluebonnet
The Rainbow Fish
Through Grandpa's Eyes
What Mary Jo Shared

We will read some of these books in class.

Expect your child to use terms like *satisfaction, talents, sharing, service, respond* and *expectations* in their conversations with you this week. You may have an opportunity to share your feelings with your child/children about *giving.* Please feel free to call with questions and concerns.

Sincerely,

Alejandro's Gift
Sometimes in Giving a Gift You Receive One as Well

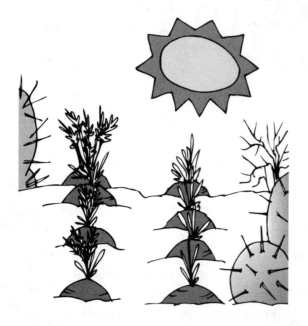

Summary

Alejandro lives in the desert and welcomes any visitor who comes along. Not many come to visit, though. To help pass the time, Alejandro plants a garden. He soon notices that when small animals come to drink water from the furrows, he isn't as lonely. He decides to help the larger animals, too, by building a watering hole. But not many animals came. Alejandro finally realizes that they need something more sheltered. A second watering hole sheltered from his house and the road is perfect. He hears the animals as they come to water and realizes that in giving, he has received a gift.

While Reading

Read to the part of the story in which Alejandro is lonelier after visitors leave than before they come.

STOP How does Alejandro feel when he is lonely? What are some things he could do to so that he would not be as lonely? Ask students what they would decide to do in his place.

Read to the point of the story in which Alejandro thinks about other animals in the desert.

STOP What are some of the things Alejandro could do for the other animals? What could happen if he does these things?

Read to the point of the story in which Alejandro finishes the watering hole, no animals come and he asks himself what he could have done incorrectly.

STOP What does Alejandro do incorrectly? How can he fix it?

Finish the story.

STOP How does Alejandro feel when he gives something to others? What does Alejandro give? What gift does he receive?

After Reading

What values do students recognize in this story? What other stories are similar to this one? How are they different? What real-life incidents touch on the same issues?

Alejandro's Gift
Extension Activities

The Desert

Locate deserts on a map. Allow students to play in the sand table, sifting, packing and digging in the sand to become familiar with it. Discuss deserts while they experience sand.

Water in the Sand

Provide two tubs, one of sand and one of dirt. Each day ask students to feel and explore the sand and dirt. Then add two cups of water. Is there a difference in the feel of the top, middle and bottom of the sand and dirt?

Ask students to plant things in each tub. Provide the same amount of water. Explore how the earth feels and how the sand feels each morning before watering.

Desert Animals

Alejandro's Gift lists many desert animals (burro, ground squirrel, wood rats, pocket gophers, jackrabbits, kangaroo rats, pocket mice, roadrunners, gilawoodpeckers, thrashers, cactus wrens, sage sparrows, mourning doves, desert tortoise, coyote, desert gray fox, bobcat, skunk, badger, long-nosed coatis, peccaries and antlered mule deer). Provide encyclopedias, animal books and picture books that show desert animals. Ask students to find pictures and information about the animals. Compare and contrast animal characteristics. Ask students to try to identify the animals in the illustrations and/or find pictures similar to those in the glossary at the end of the book.

Friendship
Giving
Perseverance
Self-Discipline
Compassion
Responsibility
Respect
Honesty

Angel Child, Dragon Child
A Story of Compassion and Understanding

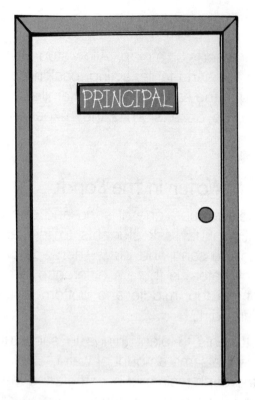

Summary

Nguyen Hoa (Ut is her at-home name) feels all alone after her move from Vietnam to the United States. Her mother stays behind when Ut, her father and siblings come to America to live. The ways of Americans are strange to her–including school, food and clothing. The children make fun of her until they get to know her. In fact, they plan a way to get her mother to the United States.

Before Reading

Ask students if they have even been any-place where people are different from them or wear different clothes. Talk about their feelings. Ask them how they feel when they are away from their parents.

While Reading

Read to the part of the story in which children make fun of Ut.

STOP What do the children say? How does Ut feel?

Read to the point of the story in which Ut and the boy have to go to the principal's office.

STOP Why are they in trouble? How does Ut feel? How does the boy feel? What could happen to them?

Read to the point of the story in which the children hear about Ut's mother.

STOP How do the children feel about all the things they have said and done to Ut?

Finish the story.

STOP How do the children and families show their caring for Ut and her family? How do the children feel? How do their families feel? How does Ut feel? How does her family feel?

After Reading

What values do students recognize in this story? What other stories are similar to this one? How are they different? What real-life incidents touch on the same issues?

Angel Child, Dragon Child
Extension Activities

Colorful Clothes

Fold a sheet of paper in half. On one half ask students to draw a picture of themselves in an outfit similar to the one Ut is shown wearing. On the other half ask them to draw a picture of themselves in what they are wearing today. Label them *School Clothes for Vietnam* and *School Clothes for (name of city and state).*

Planned Giving

Plan an activity (bake sale, used toy or clothing sale) in which children work to generate money. Save the money to give to people in the community who are in need, or give the money to an organization.

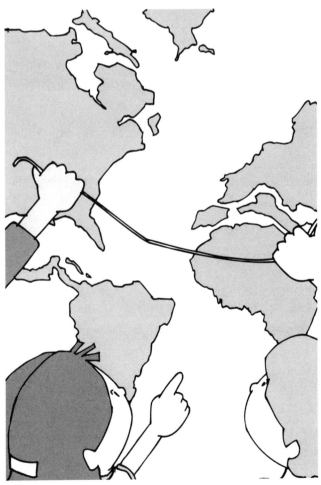

Sad and Happy

Provide students with four blank faces on a sheet of paper. Ask them to draw Ut with four different expressions on her face. Ask students to describe how Ut feels in each picture. Why does she feel that way?

Vietnam

Michele Maria Surat, the author, explains in the Afterword why the book is entitled *Angel Child, Dragon Child.* After reading the Afterword, locate Vietnam on a map. Connect it to the United States with a string. Ask students to describe how the trip might have been as they traveled to America.

The Doorbell Rang
What Can We Share?

Summary

Ma makes some cookies and allows her two children to share them. They divide them evenly. The doorbell rings. Two friends come in from next door. How do they divide the cookies now? Just when they solve the problem, the doorbell rings again and again. After splitting the cookies to one apiece, the doorbell rings again. Grandma saves the day with more cookies.

(Left margin, vertical text:) Honesty Respect Responsibility Compassion Self-Discipline Perseverance Giving Friendship

While Reading

📖 Read to the part of the story in which the doorbell rings.

🛑 What is about to happen? How do the children feel? Why? What should the children do? How will they feel? Why?

📖 Read to the point of the story in which the doorbell rings the first time, second time, etc.

🛑 Ask these questions each time the doorbell rings (until the last time): What is about to happen? How do the children feel? Why? What should the children do? How do they feel? Why?

📖 Read to the part of the story in which the doorbell rings and the children only have one cookie each.

🛑 What could happen now? How will the children feel? Why? What should the children do? How will they feel? Why?

📖 Read to the part of the story in which the doorbell rings again, for the last time.

🛑 What is about to happen? How do the children feel? Why? What should the children do? How will they feel? Why?

📖 Finish the story.

🛑 Ask students if they were able to guess what was going to happen. What should the children do? How will they feel? Why?

After Reading

What values do students recognize in this story? What other stories are similar to this one? How are they different? What real-life incidents touch on the same issues?

The Doorbell Rang
Extension Activities

Cookies for All

Provide two children with six paper cookies each. As the story is read, ask students to decide how to solve the problem before the story continues. When the story ends, make sure that all students get "real" cookies to eat while discussing the story.

Dishing Out Chips

Count the chips in several chocolate chip cookies. Record the number. Graph the results.

Prepare dough for chocolate chip cookies, leaving out the chocolate chips. Place the dough in a center. After children have washed their hands, ask them to plop dough onto a cookie sheet, count how many cookies they have and then sort chips so that each cookie has the same number of chips.

Sharing Equally

In the math center, place a bowl of flat counters to represent cookies and a bowl of craft sticks to represent people. Each child pulls out some cookies and some people. They lay the people out on the tabletop and sort the cookies so each person gets the same number. Ask students to record as many different problems as they can.

The Legend of the Bluebonnet
Will a Young Girl's Gift Save Her People?

Summary

The people of She-Who-Is-Alone ask the spirits to tell them what they must do so the drought will end. The Shaman tells them that they must make a burnt offering of their most valued possessions. When She-Who-Is-Alone realizes that her doll is her most valued possession, she knows what she must do. She throws her doll into the fire and falls asleep. In the morning the ground is covered with beautiful blue flowers, the color of the feathers in the doll's hair. The drought ends. The rains come. From that day on, She-Who-Is-Alone is known as One-Who-Dearly-Loved-Her-People.

Before Reading

Make sure students' parents will feel comfortable with their children hearing a Native American legend which tells how bluebonnets (like those found in Texas) first came to be.

While Reading

Read to the point of the story in which the people ask what they must do to bring the rain.

STOP What could the people do to get the rain to come? What can modern-day people do to get the rain to come?

Read to the point of the story in which the Shaman returns to tell his people that they must make a burnt offering.

STOP What are the valued possessions these people must give away? Ask students how they would feel if they had to give their possessions away? What are their most valued possessions?

Finish the story.

STOP How does She-Who-Is-Alone feel when she makes the decision to give away her doll? When she throws the doll into the fire? When she sees the bluebonnets? When the rains come? When she receives a new name?

After Reading

What values do students recognize in this story? What other stories are similar to this one? How are they different? What real-life incidents touch on the same issue?

The Legend of the Bluebonnet
Extension Activities

Wildflowers

Notice the wildflowers outside. What flowers cover the ground in the spring, summer and/or fall? Ask students to walk around the school to see and record the plants that are growing naturally. When they return to the room, ask them to draw a possession they value which is the same color as those plants.

Without Rain

Buy two small plants at a local greenhouse. Put them in a sunny area of the room. Water one and let the other go without "rain."

Ask each student to divide a piece of paper in half. At the top of one half, write *Rain*. At the top of the other half, write *No Rain*. Then ask the students to draw a picture of the two plants and record what happens to the one that has no rain.

A Blue Day

Send home a small piece of blue paper announcing when students will have a blue day in school. Ask them to wear something blue on that day.

Provide blue paper for assignments. Use only blue crayons or ink. Use blue paint. Use blue glue. Take a blue walk. Record blue things in blue. Provide something blue for students who may not own blue clothing.

Honesty Respect Responsibility Compassion Self-Discipline Perseverance Giving Friendship

Friendship

Giving

Perseverance

Self-Discipline

Compassion

Responsibility

Respect

Honesty

The Little Mouse, the Red Ripe Strawberry and the Big Hungry Bear
Sharing Things

Summary

Little mouse picks a big, ripe strawberry, but she is afraid the big hungry bear will eat it all. She tries hiding it, disguising it and protecting it but nothing works. Finally she decides the best thing to do is to share it with someone else.

Before Reading

Discuss how hard it can be to share when someone has something new and wonderful. What if someone is given a giant six-foot sandwich and he or she wants to keep it for themselves? Would it be possible for one person to eat that sandwich? The sandwich might end up being lost because it couldn't be used by one person. Will it spoil if it isn't eaten?

While Reading

📖 Read to the part of the story in which Little Mouse is worried.

🛑 What are the signs that Little Mouse is worried? What should Little Mouse do to keep the Bear from taking her strawberry?

📖 Read to the point of the story in which Little Mouse tries to protect her strawberry, and the storyteller says there is only one way to save it.

🛑 What should Little Mouse do now? How can she outsmart the Bear? Ask the students what they would do?

📖 Finish the story.

🛑 How does Little Mouse feel about sharing? Ask students how they can tell.

After Reading

What values do students recognize in this story? What other stories are similar to this one? How are they different? What real-life incidents touch on the same issue?

114

The Little Mouse, the Red Ripe Strawberry and the Big Hungry Bear

Extension Activities

Tea Time

Invite parents to a strawberry tea. Students can act out the story or read it as a readers' theater for entertainment. Ask students to plan the menu with as many strawberry foods as possible. Drinks could be strawberry tea or strawberry punch. Strawberry desserts or fresh fruit plates may also be served. Have students make strawberry-shaped name tags for themselves and their parents. Discuss being a good host and serving guests just like Little Mouse in the story.

Fraction Fun

Create large construction paper or card stock strawberries. Use the paper strawberries to learn how to divide in halves and quarters. Instruct students to cut the paper strawberries into four pieces. They should cut the strawberries with jagged lines instead of straight lines to create a puzzle. When they have finished, they should have a four-piece puzzle. Put the puzzles into separate envelopes with each child's name on their envelope. Ask students to share their puzzles with their classmates. Send the puzzles home so students can tell the story of Little Mouse to their families while they work the puzzle.

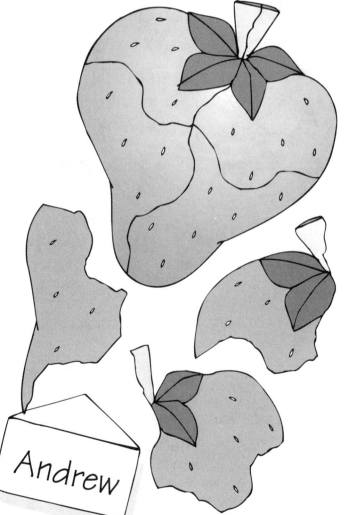

115

Name ______________________________

The Little Mouse, the Red Ripe Strawberry and the Big Hungry Bear

Word Scramble

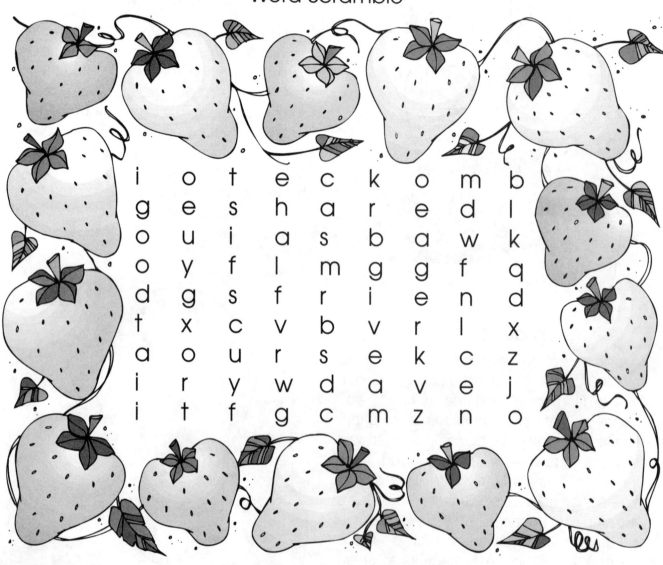

i	o	t	e	c	k	o	m	b
g	e	s	h	a	r	e	d	l
o	u	i	a	s	b	a	w	k
o	y	f	l	m	g	g	f	q
d	g	s	f	r	i	e	n	d
t	x	c	v	b	v	r	l	x
a	o	u	r	s	e	k	c	z
i	r	y	w	d	a	v	e	j
i	t	f	g	c	m	z	n	o

Find these words in the word scramble above. Look across and down.

good
eager
give
friend

shared
ours
half

Use each one of these words in a sentence about friends.

The Rainbow Fish
Giving Things Away Is Not Always Easy

Friendship

Giving

Perseverance

Self-Discipline

Compassion

Responsibility

Respect

Honesty

Summary

Rainbow Fish is a very beautiful fish with sparkling silver scales. Other fish do not have anything to do with him because he will not share his shiny scales. Rainbow Fish is upset that no one likes him and asks the wise octopus for advice.

Before Reading

Discuss the cover. Talk about the beautiful fish and predict how he got his name. As each page of the story is finished, pause to let children "ooo and ah" at the illustrations.

While Reading

📖 Read to the part of the story in which the little blue fish asks for a shiny scale.

🛑 Why does the little blue fish want one of the shiny scales? Will Rainbow Fish give him one? Why? Why not?

📖 Read to the point of the story in which the starfish tells him to go to the wise octopus.

🛑 Why is Rainbow Fish so lonely? Even though Rainbow Fish is beautiful, why don't the other fish like him? Predict what advice the wise octopus will give him.

📖 Read to the point of the story in which the advice is given by the wise octopus.

🛑 What is the problem Rainbow Fish faces? What advice does the wise octopus give Rainbow Fish? Are there any other ways to solve this problem? Why does Rainbow Fish say he could not be happy without all his shining scales? Predict whether Rainbow Fish will take the advice from the wise octopus.

📖 Finish the story.

🛑 What are the prized possessions of Rainbow Fish? Why does giving his shiny scales away make him happy? Ask students how they would feel if they were one of the other fish? Ask if they have ever been in a situation where they have felt good about sharing? Ask what would happen if students lost their friends because they wouldn't share?

After Reading

What values do students recognize in this story? What other stories are similar to this one? How are they different? What real-life incidents touch on the same issues?

The Rainbow Fish
Extension Activities

Bubbles About Sharing

Make a mural of brightly colored fish on blue paper. Use foil to add shiny scales. Some students may wish to add other plants, sand and shells to the mural.

Draw air bubbles above the fish. Ask students to copy phrases from the book that the fish says about sharing. Ask students to make up some of their own, too.

I Can Share, Too

Ask students to think of something they can do really well. Write it on a piece of paper. Glue foil on the back of the paper. Ask students to share their skills with others. Pair up students. Ask one student to say to another something like, "I think I can draw dinosaurs really well. Would you like me to help you learn to draw them?"

Rainbow Giving Poem

Ask students to write the word RAINBOW, using a different color of the rainbow for each letter (red, orange, yellow, green, blue, blue-violet, violet). Ask students to work in groups and think of words about sharing or giving that start with each letter.

After each letter, tell students to write a word that describes *giving* or *sharing* that starts with that letter. For example, after the red "R," they can write *Receive* in red.

Related Readings

Read the story *What Mary Jo Shared* by J.M. Udry.

Bibliography

Albert, R.E. (1994). *Alejandro's Gift.* San Francisco: Chronicle Books. ISBN: 0-8118-1342-8

Bunting, Eve. (1988). *How Many Days to America?* New York: Clarion Books. ISBN: 0-395-54777-6

De Paola, Tomie. (1983). *The Legend of the Bluebonnet.* New York: G.P. Putnam's Sons. ISBN: 00-399-20938-7

Hutchins, P. (1986). *The Doorbell Rang.* New York: Mulberry Books. ISBN: 0-688-09234-9

Hutchins, P. (1986). *The Doorbell Rang.* (audiocassette). Blackstone Audio Books.

MacLachlan, Patricia. (1979). *Through Grandpa's Eyes.* New York: Harper & Row Publishers. ISBN: 0-06-024044X

Pfister, Marcus. (1992). *The Rainbow Fish.* New York: North–South Books, Inc. ISBN: 1-55858-009-3

Surat, Michele Maria. (1983). *Angel Child, Dragon Child.* New York: Scholastic, Inc. ISBN: 0-590-42271-5

Udry, J.M. (1966). *What Mary Jo Shared.* Chicago, IL: A. Whitman.

Udry, J.M. (1982). *What Mary Jo Shared.* (videocassette). Pasadena, CA: Barr Films.

Wood, Don and Audrey. (1989). *The Little Mouse, the Red Ripe Strawberry and the Big Hungry Bear.* Child's Play. ISBN: 0-85953-012-4

119

Dear Parents,

This week we are studying about *friendship*, one of the virtues that Dr. J. William Bennett suggests we examine. Dr. Boyer defines *friendship* as "Friendship usually rises out of mutual interests and common aims, and these pursuits are strengthened by the benevolent impulses that sooner or later grow. The demands of friendship–for frankness, for self-revelation, for taking friends' criticisms as seriously as their expressions of admiration or praise, for stand-by-me-loyalty, and for assistance to the point of self-sacrifice–are all potent encouragements to moral maturation and even ennoblement." Dr. William J. Bennett was Secretary of Education and Chairman of the National Endowment for the Humanities under President Reagan and Director of the Office of National Drug Control Policy during the Bush Administration. His books, *The Book of Virtues*, and *The Book of Virtues for Young People*, are widely acclaimed.

Several books for young children address *friendship*. These include:

Arthur's Baby
The Berenstain Bears Get in a Fight
Fast Friends: A Tail and Tongue Tale
Frog and Toad Books
The Great White Man-Eating Shark: A Cautionary Tale
Jamaica and Brianna
It's Mine
Max and Ruby's Midas: Another Greek Myth
No Fighting, No Biting!
Three Wishes
Two Good Friends
The Velveteen Rabbit

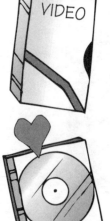

We will read some of these in class.

Expect your child/children to use terms like *satisfaction*, *talents*, *sharing*, *service*, *respond* and *expectations* in their conversations with you this week. You may have an opportunity to share your feelings with your child/children about *friendship*. Please feel free to call me with questions and concerns.

Sincerely,

120

The Berenstain Bears Get in a Fight
A Storm and a Rainbow

Summary

Brother Bear wakes up in a very bad mood. He and Sister Bear get into a argument which escalates and lasts all day. Finally, Mother Bear gets tired of hearing them argue and explains that even folks who love each other sometimes get into fights. When the two little Bears realize that fighting and making up are part of living together, they decide to make up and have fun together.

Before Reading

Discuss students' feelings when they have an argument with someone they care about. How do they feel? Is it easy to make up with that person? Why is it so hard to apologize and make up?

While Reading

Read to the part of the story in which the reason for the fight between Brother Bear and Sister Bear becomes apparent.

STOP Why does Sister Bear take so long getting ready? How does Brother Bear react?

Read to the part of the story in which Brother and Sister do unfriendly things to each other that day.

STOP Are Brother and Sister having fun? How do they feel about their argument? What do they do and say that shows how they feel?

Finish the story.

STOP How does Mama describe a rainbow? How is a rainbow like a person's feelings when making up after a fight?

After Reading

What values do students recognize in this story? What other stories are similar to this one? How are they different? What real-life incidents touch on the same issue?

The Berenstain Bears Get in a Fight
Extension Activities

Art Activity

Ask students to draw a line down the middle of a sheet of paper. Then ask them to draw Brother and Sister on one half of the paper. Label this part of the picture, *The Storm.* On the other half of the paper, Brother and Sister should be playing happily. A rainbow should be in the picture. Label this half of the picture, *The Rainbow.*

Making Up

Ask students to help Brother Bear finish this letter to Sister Bear.

Dear Sister,

This was a very _____ day.

I am sorry we _____

_____

_____

I would like to _____

_____

_____

Then we can _____

_____

_____

Sincerely,

Brother

Related Readings

Other books about getting along are *Arthur's Baby* by Marc Brown and *No Fighting, No Biting!* by Else Holmelund Minarik.

122

What's the Opposite?

Read the word in the column on the left. Think of a word that is the opposite of that word.
Write the word in the box on the right.

Check your answers with a friend. Do you have the same words? Are you both right?

Word	**Opposite**
storm	
angry	
fight	
share	
shout	

What other words can you think of that tell about anger and fighting? List them on the
back of this sheet. Can you think of opposites, too?

Friendship Giving Perseverance Self-Discipline Compassion Responsibility Respect Honesty

Fast Friends: A Tail and Tongue Tale
Getting Along Makes Things Easier

Summary

A cow and a chameleon become friends and decide to live together. Blueberry Spring, the cow, is a total slob. Smithfield, the chameleon, is a neat freak. This odd couple overcome their differences and live happily ever after.

While Reading

📖 Read to the part of the story in which the cow and chameleon become friends and move to the city where their favorite activity is bug thwakking.

🛑 How does bug thwakking satisfy the friendship? Recall their jobs in the city. What things do they do together as friends when they get home from their jobs?

📖 Finish the story.

🛑 What are some of Blueberry Spring's old habits that are hard to break? Are old habits hard to break? Why? Why not? What event causes Smithfield to pack his bags and leave? How does Blueberry Spring feel about being separated from Smithfield? How does Smithfield feel about being separated from Blueberry Spring? How do they resolve their differences and become roommates again? What other alternatives would help resolve their differences?

After Reading

What values do students recognize in this story? What other stories are similar to this one? How are they different? What real-life incidents touch on the same issue?

124

Fast Friends: A Tail and Tongue Tale
Extension Activities

Both Positive and Negative

Use chart paper to study the positive and negative traits of each character in the story. Some of the literature reproducibles at the end of this book may help.

Blueberry Spring		Smithfield	
+	**−**	**+**	**−**
good writer	spills popcorn	good cook	nags

Helpers Together

Generate a helper chart for the classroom. Ask students to work together on tasks instead of each person having a specific task to do alone. After a week of working together instead of alone, discuss the positive and negative aspects about working together.

Let's Get Together

Generate a list of two animals or people who are unlikely partners but overcome their differences and get along. Example: A rhino and a bird who feeds off his back.

Pair Share

Fold a sheet of paper into fourths. Ask students to draw a picture of something they like to do in each fourth. Then ask them to cut out each picture. Pair students. Ask them to match the pictures each had that are alike. Put the other pictures in a stack together. Each pair of children should join another pair and see what happens with all the different things they like to do.

Related Readings

Two other good books about friendship are *Two Good Friends* by J. Delton and *Frog and Toad Are Friends* by Arnold Lobel.

It's Mine
Quarreling Hurts Everyone

Summary

Three quarrelsome frogs shout "It's mine!" from dawn to dusk. A large toad tells them the bickering has to stop. But the quarreling continues until one day it rains so much the frogs are in danger. They cling to a rock while they wait for the flood to subside. The rock turns out to be the toad. The three frogs soon live together in peace.

Before Reading

Discuss the meaning of a fable. It is a short story, usually with animals as the characters, that teaches a lesson called a moral.

While Reading

📖 Read to the part of the story in which Lydia leaps to catch a butterfly.

🛑 What are some of the hateful things the frogs say to each other? Identify the problem. Discuss the problems that may continue. What could they do to solve the problem?

📖 Read to the point of the story in which the toad hops away through the weeds.

🛑 How does the large toad feel about his neighbors? What does he tell the frogs? Predict whether or not the frogs will stop bickering. Why?

📖 Read to the point of the story in which the rain stops.

🛑 Do the frogs listen to the large toad? What do they do? Discuss the expressions on the frogs' faces. What will happen next? Ask students to justify their predictions.

📖 Turn to the page and allow time for students to see the large rock. Then finish the story.

🛑 Have the frogs changed? If so, how? What is the moral of the story?

After Reading

What values do students recognize in this story? What other stories are similar to this one? How are they different? What real-life incidents touch on the same issue?

It's Mine
Extension Activities

What Is a Fable?

Review the story by discussing the moral of the fable. Recall other fables you have read or select others to share, such as *Fables* by Arnold Lobel. Write the moral of each fable in a one-sentence statement. Post the morals as *Words of Wisdom* on a bulletin board.

Artists

Outline the story into enough events so that students can work in small groups to illustrate each page of a class big book. Use torn paper pieces for scenery. Frogs can be assembled by cutting the body parts and gluing them together. Refer students to Lionni's style. Explain that as a child, Lionni taught himself to draw by copying artwork in museums. Summarize the story to be written on each page. Use the class big book so students can retell the story.

A New Class Pet

Find an aquarium. It can be old and even cracked since it does not need to hold water. Ask students what is needed to prepare the container for a frog. This may result in some research. Arrange a field trip to a local pet store to purchase a frog and the necessary items for a frog's new home. When the new class pet arrives, develop plans for its care.

Related Readings

Try reading *The Great White Man-Eating Shark: A Cautionary Tale* by Margaret Mahy.

Jamaica and Brianna
Whose Boots Do You Like?

Giving

Perseverance

Self-Discipline

Compassion

Responsibility

Respect

Honesty

Summary

Jamaica does not want to wear her brother's old boots because Brianna has pink boots. When Jamaica gets new boots, she makes fun of Brianna's boots. Each girl hurts the other's feelings about their boots. When they finally talk about their feelings, they learned that each likes the other's boots.

Before Reading

Discuss the feelings of jealousy when a friend gets something new. Why do people sometimes feel badly when they should be excited for a friend's good fortune? How can those feelings be dealt with? How does talking about feelings help?

While Reading

📖 Read to the part of the story in which Jamaica tears her brother's gray boots.

🛑 Why doesn't Jamaica's mother just buy her new boots? How does Brianna hurt Jamaica's feelings? What could she say differently?

📖 Read to the point of the story in which Brianna tells Jamaica that cowboy boots are "in."

🛑 What does Brianna mean when she says cowboy boots aren't in? Who decides what is in and what is not? Why does Brianna say that to Jamaica?

📖 Finish the story.

🛑 What reason does Jamaica give for saying Brianna's boots are ugly? How do the two girls solve their misunderstanding?

After Reading

What values do students recognize in this story? What other stories are similar to this one? How are they different? What real-life incidents touch on the same issues?

Jamaica and Brianna
Extension Activities

Recycling

Invite a speaker from a local charity such as a goodwill store or a second-hand clothing store to visit your class. Ask the speaker to tell why people may need or want to wear used clothes. Discuss why it is important not to throw away things that are still usable. Ask students and their families to donate clothing items that can be taken to a charity and recycled for others to use.

In and Out!

Bring old magazines and pictures to school to show how fashions change. Discuss why people sometimes throw away good clothes and buy new ones just to feel "in." Talk about how silly those same clothes look later, when they are "out." What happens to those old clothes? Discuss the impact on the environment when clothes, blankets, boots and shoes are recycled. Discuss how it is possible to enjoy someone else's used things.

Our Compliments

Write a complimentary sticky note for each student. Discuss how it makes students feel to receive the compliments. If compliments make people feel good, why don't people compliment each other more often?

Three Wishes
Maybe Friendship Is the Most Important Thing

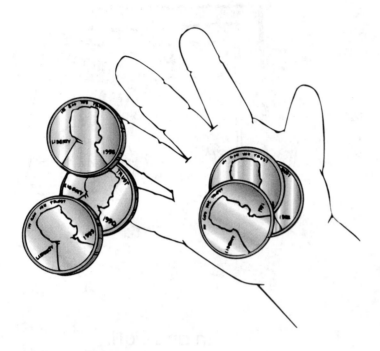

Summary

On New Year's Day, Nobie finds a penny with her birth date on it. She and her friend, Victoria, decide it means she will be granted three wishes. When her wishes start to come true, Nobie discovers that the best wish is for a good friend.

Before Reading

Discuss other stories about making a wish. Aladdin is a popular example. Talk about what students would wish for if they had three wishes. What does the saying, "Be careful what you wish for" mean? What could make a wish go wrong?

While Reading

Read to the part of the story in which Nobie's first wish comes true.

STOP What are some of the reasons the sun comes out? Does the sun really come out because Nobie wishes it to be warmer? What does the word *coincidence* mean? Could this be a coincidence?

Read to the point of the story in which Nobie makes her second wish.

STOP What is Nobie angry about? Why does Nobie wish Victor would leave? What is she really angry about? Does Nobie really mean to make the wish? What could she have done differently? What should be the final wish?

Finish the story.

STOP Why does Mama say that she would wish for good friends? Why are friends important? What does Victor do that makes him such a good friend?

After Reading

What values do students recognize in this story? What other stories are similar to this one? How are they different? What real-life incidents touch on the same issue?

Three Wishes
Extension Activities

Collecting Coins

Ask students to collect pennies minted in the year of their birth and bring them to school. Put the pennies in a money jar or piggy bank. Some students may wish to bring in pennies dated each year from the year of their birth. Discuss groups and organizations that make wishes come true. When the collection of pennies builds up, ask students to decide which organization should get their pennies.

Three Wishes for My Family

Fold a sheet of paper lengthwise into three boxes. At the top write *Three Wishes for My Family*. Ask students to wish for things to give to their families by drawing the wish in a box.

Mount the pictures on a larger piece of construction paper and draw faces in the border or decorate the border with faces of people from magazines.

Make a List

Ask students to help make a list of the qualities in a good friend. Display the list where everyone can see it. When a student does something that is on the list, point it out to the child and place a smiley face sticker next to the quality.

The Velveteen Rabbit
A Special Friendship

Summary

A beloved stuffed rabbit becomes real to the boy in this story. When the boy falls ill, the Velveteen Rabbit stays with him until he is well. When the boy recovers, the doctor orders Velveteen Rabbit to be destroyed because it is "a mess of . . . germs." The nursery magic fairy saves Velveteen Rabbit by changing it into a real rabbit so it can escape.

Before Reading

Discuss why some toys become favorites. What kinds of toys became special? Discuss the comfort a stuffed animal or blanket can be when a person is sick or sad.

While Reading

Read to the part of the story in which Velveteen Rabbit is so special that it becomes real.

STOP Discuss the difference between fantasy stories in which the animals become real only when people aren't around and a stuffed animal that seems real to a child all the time. How does Skin Horse describe becoming real? Does it happen suddenly? Does it happen only when the lights are out and the people are asleep? Ask students how a person can tell if a toy has become real.

Read to the point of the story in which the boy and Velveteen Rabbit become friends.

STOP What kinds of things do the boy and the Velveteen Rabbit do together? What qualities do they have to offer each other? What makes a good friend? What are some ways people can be better friends to others?

Read to the point of the story in which the boy recovers and the doctor orders Velveteen Rabbit destroyed.

STOP Discuss the seriousness of scarlet fever and why belongings need to be cleaned or destroyed. Reassure students that scarlet fever is now treated with better medication and care. Why are the doctor and Nana afraid to let the boy play with Velveteen Rabbit? How do germs get passed around? Why is Velveteen Rabbit so sad to be forgotten? What does it feel like to be pushed aside by his friend?

Finish the story.

STOP How does Velveteen Rabbit make new friends? Why is it shy at first?

After Reading

What values do students recognize in this story? What other stories are similar to this one? How are they different? What real-life incidents touch on the same issue?

132

The Velveteen Rabbit
Extension Activities

Making a Rabbit Book

Use heavy paper for the pages in the book. Punch two or three holes along the side of each piece of paper. Provide pieces of fabric that have different textures and patterns. Give each student a rabbit stencil to trace over the piece of fabric chosen by that child. Cut out the rabbit shape and draw a face on the rabbit. Glue on buttons for eyes and a cotton ball for a tail. Label each page with the student's name. Use ring binders or yarn to put the book together.

Unusual Friends

Make a list of students' favorite stories about friends. Ask students to help list as many characters as possible who are good examples of friends. List the characteristics of the friendship besides each of the friends. Use this list to write a sentence describing a good friend.

Real and Fantasy

Ask students to help make two lists comparing and contrasting Velveteen Rabbit with a real rabbit.

In one list, write characteristics that are used to describe Velveteen Rabbit. Reread passages that will help students describe this special character. In the other list, write characteristics of real rabbits. In what ways are they alike? Different?

Bibliography

Berenstain, Stan. (1982). *The Berenstain Bears Get in a Fight.* (with CD-ROM). New York: Random House. ISBN: 0-394-85132-3

Brown, M.T. (1990). *Arthur's Baby.* Boston: Joy Street Books. ISBN: 0-316-11007-8

Clifton, Lucille. (1992). *Three Wishes.* New York: Dell Publishing. ISBN: 0-440-40921-7

Delton, J. (1974). *Two Good Friends.* New York: Crown Publishers.

Havill, Juanita. (1993). *Jamaica and Brianna.* Boston, Houghton Mifflin Company. ISBN: 0-395-64489-5

Horstman, Lisa. (1994). *Fast Friends: A Tail and Tongue Tale.* New York: Alfred A. Knopf, Inc. ISBN: 0-679-85404-5

Lionni, Leo. (1995). *It's Mine.* New York: Scholastic. ISBN: 0-590-62198-X

Lobel, A. (1985). *Arnold Lobel Video Showcase.* (videocassette). Westminster, MD: Random House School Division.

Lobel, A. (1980). *Fables.* New York: Harper & Row. ISBN: 0-06-023974

Lobel, A. (1987). *Frog and Toad.* New York: Harper & Row.

Lobel, A. (1976). *Frog and Toad All Year.* New York: Harper & Row. ISBN: 0-06-023951-4

Lobel, A. (1985). *Frog and Toad All Year.* (audiocassette). New York: Listening Library.

Lobel, A. (1985). *Frog and Toad Are Friends.* (audiocassette). New York: Caedmon.

Lobel, A. (1985). *Frog and Toad Together.* (audiocassette). New York: Listening Library

Lobel, A. (1972). *Frog and Toad Together.* New York: Harper & Row. ISBN: 0-06-023960-3

Mahy, M. (1990). *The Great White Man-Eating Shark: A Cautionary Tale.* New York: Dial Books for Young Readers. ISBN: 0-8037-0749-5

Minarik, E.H. (1958). *No Fighting, No Biting!* New York: Harper. ISBN: 0-06-024291-4

Wells, Rosemary. (1995). *Max and Ruby's Midas: Another Greek Myth.* New York: Penguin Books. ISBN: 0-8037-1782-2

Williams, Margery. (1975). *The Velveteen Rabbit.* Ill. William Nicholson. New York: Doubleday and Company, Inc. ISBN: 0-380-43257-9 (Many editions available.)

Williams, Margery. (1975). *The Velveteen Rabbit.* (audiocassette). New York: Simon & Schuster Juvenile.

The Velveteen Rabbit. Toucan Software. (1993). (CD-ROM). Queue, Inc.

134

Children's Literature Organizers

Using the Reproducibles

The reproducibles on these pages can be used with any of the stories in this book. Use the material by copying it directly, making an overhead transparency, enlarging it on a chart or re-creating it on the chalkboard. Children learn through a variety of styles. By using graphic organizers, children can visualize the discussion and participate in creating the ideas.

For clearer comprehension, use different colored markers for each part of the display. The information may be written on the chart or written on other paper and added to the chart. The second method allows for the information to be manipulated, changed and rearranged as a discussion proceeds. Use simple illustrations for enhanced understanding or to add color and decoration. Select the reproducible that will emphasize the objective of the lesson. Overuse of the reproducibles lessens their effect.

Comparing Stories

Choose two stories that illustrate the same value. Write the title of each story at the top of the page. Guide the discussion and record the information from students in each space. Use the guiding questions at the bottom of the summary pages for discussion. Older students can complete the chart in small groups or individually. After completing this activity, students should understand that problems can be solved in a variety of ways.

Solving Problems

Ask students to identify the problem at the beginning of the story and write it in a brief statement. Discuss events that happen in the story as the characters try to solve the problem. List each event separately on the chart. The numbers of events will vary with each story. Discussion should lead to the solution of the problem. Write the solution. This activity helps students identify the story's problem and solution. It also helps teach story sequencing and summarization.

Plot Chart

The plot shows students the progress of the story as it moves toward a solution. After completing the chart, ask students to identify the value(s) illustrated in the story. Summarize the discussion into a single statement. The information on the plot chart will help create the summary statement. Use the plot chart with a whole group, a small group or as an independent activity.

Agree/Disagree

As students critically discuss the value in each story, some will agree with the characters' solutions, and others will disagree. This chart will help students think critically about the options available to the characters and hopefully to themselves if they are involved in similar incidents. Write specific statements from the story in the first column. As students discuss a statement, record their opinions in the Agree and Disagree columns. Be sure that students justify their opinions before they are recorded on the chart. Students should realize that all opinions are acceptable as long as they reflect their own feelings or beliefs. This activity will strengthen students' ability to verbalize feelings.

Story Web

A story web helps students recall and understand elements of a story and the relationships between the elements. The *setting* should include the time and place of the story. Draw a line out from the *setting* circle. At the end of the line draw a box labeled *time*. Draw another line from the *setting* circle. Add a box labeled *place*. Draw additional lines from the boxes for more details: large city, park, sandpile, etc. Characters are listed as major and/or minor. Draw a line out from the *character* circle for each character. Put a circle or box at the end of the line. Write the character's name in the box. Draw lines from each character circle and label the traits of each character. Continue with *plot* and *theme* circles. Story webs can be very simple and brief, or as students gain experience with webs, they may add more detailed information.

Story Map

Make a story map to help students recall and understand important elements of the story. The story setting should include the time and place of the story. Characters can be listed as major and/or minor, depending on each story. Traits of each character may also be listed. The plot includes the major events of the story. The theme is a summary of the plot and encompasses the value(s) identified in the story.

Story Frame

A story frame helps students understand the elements of story grammar. Stories have a beginning, middle and end. Target words such as *in the beginning* and *finally* give students clues in recalling the story sequence. Beginning writers will find a story frame helpful in writing the story in their own words. The frame can be adjusted to the number of events in the story or to more specific information in each story. Add character names to help students retell the story.

136

Comparing Stories

	1.	2.
Main Character		
Other Characters		
Setting		
Problem		
Solution		

How are the stories alike? _____

_____

_____

How are the stories different? _____

_____

_____

Which story do you like best? Why? _____

_____

_____

Solving Problems

Problem: _____

_____

_____

_____

Event 1: _____

_____

_____

_____

Event 2: _____

_____

_____

_____

Event 3: _____

_____

_____

_____

Solution: _____

_____

_____

_____

138

Plot Chart

Characters: _____

_____

_____

Setting: _____

_____

_____

Problem: _____

_____

_____

Events: _____

_____

_____

Ending: _____

_____

_____

Values brought out in story: _____

_____

_____

_____

_____

Agree/Disagree Chart

Statement	Agree	Disagree

Story Web

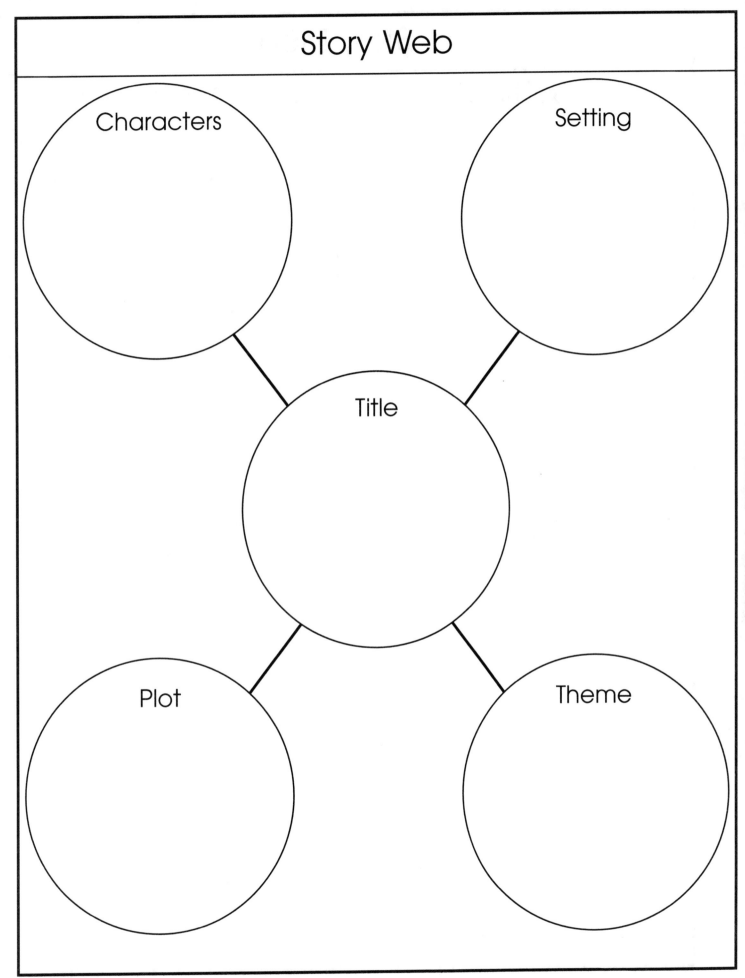

Characters

Setting

Title

Plot

Theme

Story Map

Setting

Characters

Plot

Theme

Story Frame

In the beginning, _____

_____

_____

_____

_____

Then _____

_____

_____

_____

_____

And _____

_____

_____

_____

_____

Finally, _____

_____

_____

_____

_____

Teacher Resources

American Library Association's Notable Children's Books. World Wide Web: http://www.ala.org/alaorg/alsc/notbooks.html#Younger.

Bennett, W.J. (1995). Ill. Michael Hague. *The Children's Book of Virtues.* Oregon: Harvest House. ISBN: 1-56507-329-0

Bennett, W.J. (1995). *The Moral Compass: Stories for a Life's Journey.* New York: Simon & Schuster.

Bennett, W.J. (1995). *The Book of Virtues.* New York: Silver Burdett Press. ISBN: 0-382-24923-2

Boyer, E.L. (1995). *The Basic School: A Community for Learning.* Princeton, NJ: The Carnegie Foundation for the Advancement of Teaching.

Conan, D., S. Palomares, and D. Schilling. (1992). *Teaching the Skills of Conflict Resolution.* Spring Valley, CA: Innerchoice Publishing.

Essa, E. (1990). *A Practical Guide to Solving Preschool Behavior Problems* (2nd ed.). New York: Delmar.

Fields, M.V., and C. Boesser. (1994). *Constructive Guidance and Discipline: Preschool and Primary Education.* New York: Macmillan Publishing Company.

Johnson, D.W., and R.T. Johnson. (1995). *Reducing School Violence Through Conflict Resolution.* Alexandria, VA: Association for Supervision and Curriculum Development (ASCD).

Kilpatrick, W., G. Wolfe, and S. Wolfe. (1994). *Books That Build Character.* New York: Simon & Schuster.

McBee, R.H. (1996). "Can Controversial Topics Be Taught in the Early Grades? The Answer Is Yes!" *Social Education (The Official Journal of National Council for the Social Studies),* 60(1), pp. 38-41.

Publishers Weekly Children's Bestseller List. World Wide Web: http://www.bookwire.com/pw/bsl/chilrens/current.childrens.htmi#picture.

Rasinski, T., and C. Gillespie. (1992). *Sensitive Issues: An Annotated Guide to Children's Literature,* K-6. Oryx Press.

Sockett, H. (1996). "Can Virtue Be Taught?" *The Educational Forum (Kappa Delta Pi),* 60(2), pp. 124-129.

Sorenson, D.L. (1992). *Conflict Resolution and Mediation for Peer Helpers.* Minneapolis, MN: Educational Media Corporation.